Business Roles

John Crowther-Alwyn

D1478113

CAMBRIDGE
UNIVERSITY PRESS

PUBLISHED BY THE PRESS SYNDICATE OF THE UNIVERSITY OF CAMBRIDGE
The Pitt Building, Trumpington Street, Cambridge CB2 1RP, United Kingdom

CAMBRIDGE UNIVERSITY PRESS
The Edinburgh Building, Cambridge CB2 2RU, United Kingdom
40 West 20th Street, New York, NY 10011–4211, USA
10 Stamford Road, Oakleigh, Melbourne 3166, Australia

First published 1997
Reprinted 1997

Printed in the United Kingdom at the University Press, Cambridge

ISBN 0 521 46953 8

Contents

Thanks and acknowledgements

Author's acknowledgements

I dedicate this book to my mother.

I wish to thank: France, Anthony, Laura and Chloé for their patience while I wrote this book; Diane Owen, Micky Ashton, Alan Reed and Gillian Michl for their help and advice; Will Capel and Sarah Almy of CUP for their immense competence and professionalism; all my students, especially those at CEAC and L'Ecole Supérieure de Finances in Cergy-Pontoise, for their enthusiastic participation in the simulations.

The author and publishers would like to thank the following individuals and institutions for their help in piloting and commenting on the material and for the invaluable feedback which they provided:

Cait Hardie, Suzanne Mead, Gillian Neeley and Marleen Reibel-Baeten, Insearch Language Centre, Sydney, Australia; Will Sykes, the Bell Language School, Cambridge, England; Peter Lake, International House, Toulouse, France; Sarah Jones-Macziola, International House, Freiburg, Germany; Gaynor MacGregor and Philip Moore, Cambridge Institut, Munich, Germany; Barbara Chilvers, British Council, Hong Kong; Andy Cresswell, British Institute of Florence, Florence, Italy; Simon Williams, International House, Kielce, Poland; Tim Bright, Garanti Bank Training Centre, Istanbul, Turkey; David Cordell, Eurocentre, Alexandria, USA.

The author and publishers are grateful to the following copyright owners for permission to reproduce copyright material. Every endeavour has been made to contact copyright owners and apologies are expressed for any omissions:

p 22 Sony United Kingdom Ltd, Rolex Watch Co Ltd, Reebok (© 1995 Reebok International Ltd. All Rights Reserved. Reebok and ▆ are Registered Trademarks of Reebok International), Ford Motor Company, Chanel and ⓒ are registered trademarks of Chanel Ltd, IBM, IBM is the registered trademark of International Business machines Corporation.

The author and publishers are grateful to the following illustrators and photographic sources:

p 23 Colorific/ Matrix; Telegraph Colour Library, pages 31, 46, 54 (photographers: Bonnington, Rowell, McCormick); p 38 Kelly Holmes by Neale Haynes, Allsport UK Ltd; p 62 Matassa/ Ace; p 71 Eriksson/ Camera Press; p 78 J. Allan Cash Photo Library; p 85 Abrahams/ Network; p 92 Doherty/ Image Bank

Book designed by MetaDesign London.

Introduction

What is *Business Roles*?

Business Roles is a photocopiable resource book containing 12 simulations for students of Business English.

It is designed to enable learners to participate in lively and interesting discussions about a wide variety of business topics, and to develop fluency and other communication skills for their jobs.

In each simulation, learners participate in a meeting, using prescribed roles, discuss an important matter and try to come to a decision.

The material has three important features:

- it tells learners what their opinions are about the matter being debated. This enables them to concentrate on their communication skills rather than having to make up opinions about the matter in question. Disagreement is built into the roles to ensure that real discussion does take place

- it is concise. Little time need be devoted to preparation and assimilation of facts and figures

- all the situations are authentic, but real names and trademarks are left out of the main debate to enable learners to get away from their real-life roles and companies. They are also international in focus, presenting a range of business situations in a range of countries

Business Roles are communicative situations: the main result of learners using them is a development of fluency through meaningful exchange. *Business Roles* is not a coursebook: it does not offer structured input, and the only specific language work is in the follow-up feedback stage (where opportunity is given for both self and peer analysis in a variety of ways). Rather it is a practice book, designed to activate the learner's language and develop their communication skills.

Each simulation can be preceded by an introductory task which familiarises learners with the topic to be discussed and the vocabulary to be used.

Complete and user-friendly teacher's notes are provided at the beginning of the book to make it clear and easy for teachers to understand how to go about using the introductory task, the preparatory phase, the simulation, and the follow-up. Each simulation also has its own detailed guidance and background information to facilitate the teacher's task.

All the pages intended for the learners (preparatory task, situation, roles, and follow-up questions) can be photocopied.

Who is *Business Roles* for?

These simulations can be used with pre- and post-experience learners at intermediate level and above, in groups of three upwards. If you like to have distinctive 'input' and 'output' phases, use these simulations in the output phase. Likewise, if you have 'study' and 'practice' phases, they are ideally suited to the 'practice' part.

You can use the book on its own, but it is ideal as a complement to a coursebook or other teaching materials.

Business Roles is particularly well adapted to courses in business English, but will be enjoyed by anyone who is going to work, works, or has worked, in industry, services or commerce.

The key points of *Business Roles*

- Simplicity: they are easy to use for learners and teachers. The basic format is always the same: the participants have the 'situation', which gives basic facts about the company and the question to be discussed, and their own individual role, with details of their job in the firm and their opinions.

- Clarity: there is usually only one main problem to be solved and it is always quite clear what it is.

- Brevity: while all essential information is provided, you won't need a lengthy preparation time. The main debate can last anything from 30 to 75 minutes.

- Authenticity: the roles and the firms involved are fictional, but reflect real debates in real companies, and are backed up with a variety of data to create realistic and credible situations.

- Fun: there is a lighthearted element in many of these roles. An effort has been made to avoid the slightly over-serious atmosphere sometimes found in business material.

- Communication: these roles will encourage your learners to get involved in the discussion.

- Flexibility: the situations can be used with a variety of learners and class sizes. Furthermore, each time you use a situation with a group, the outcome of the discussion is potentially different: they are open, and leave room for imagination.

- Variety: many aspects of business life are covered, from marketing to product development, from communication to personnel management in a variety of types of company, in different countries, with all sorts of problems. What's more, learners can have a different 'job' each time – CEO one day, Marketing Manager the next.

- Participation: the way the roles are designed makes it difficult for learners not to join in at some point.

General notes for teachers

The structure of the simulations

Each simulation has four distinct phases:

1. Introduction: this is designed as an introduction to the subject in general, not to the specific questions raised in the simulation itself. It takes the form of a discussion, or an activity designed to provoke discussion. It is optional, but highly recommended in some cases.

2. Preparation: this is preparation of the simulation itself. Each preparation takes the form of reading through the situation and individual roles, and individual preparation.

3. The simulation itself: this is based on a 'situation' describing the issues to be debated, and a 'role' for each learner.

4. Follow-up: this is not compulsory, but it can provide a very useful evaluation of how the meeting went and of group and individual performances. Note-taking during the roleplay/simulation, the use of a video camera to record and then review the meeting, and individual evaluation sheets can all provide a wealth of information on what went well and what didn't (if anything), and how to make things even better in the next discussion.

How to use each simulation

The tasks in the introductory phase vary with each simulation, and detailed teacher's notes are given within the simulation. For the preparatory and follow-up phases, and the meeting itself, the following approach is suggested for all the simulations:

Preparation

1. Give out the photocopies with any other material such as maps or fact sheets, to your learners.

2. Read the situation through together and answer any questions about vocabulary or about the facts of the situation itself. The vocabulary lists supplied in the teacher's notes for each situation are designed to give a handy definition of the words and phrases your learners are most likely to ask you about. Also included is some useful background information for teachers and students unfamiliar with the issue under discussion. If necessary, ask some comprehension questions about the situation, to ensure everyone understands it.

3. Draw learners' particular attention to the question(s) to be discussed in the box at the end of the situation. This is not in the form of an agenda, but does constitute one.

4. Give out the individual roles. The roles are lettered and 'A' is the most essential: the later in the alphabet the role's letter, the less essential it is to the discussion. 'A' is always the President/CEO/Managing Director, and is always the chair.

5. Let each participant read through their role and answer any questions they may have.

6. Set aside a preparation period. This can quite well be done for homework: alternatively, if you have a large class, and so several discussion groups, learners with the same role can prepare together. Learners will prepare their roles, noting down, if they so wish, what they are going to say. Encourage them to anticipate the other participants' arguments as well.

7. Before beginning the meeting, ask all participants to say exactly what their jobs are and where they work. (This is information which 'real' participants would know before the meeting, and it is important to separate this brief phase from the actual discussion.)

The simulation

Begin the main discussion. Leave the chairperson to chair the meeting: he or she will have instructions about how to do this on their role card. Intervene as little as possible. Film participants or take notes to use in follow-up (see sections below).

Remember that there is never one 'right' answer to resolve the problem: the outcome will depend very much on each group. Students who have done case studies for marketing or business studies, where there is sometimes an imposed result, may find this puzzling, but it is much more realistic.

Follow-up

See sections below on 'Taking feedback notes', 'The use of a cassette recorder', 'The use of video' and 'Learner follow-up and evaluation'.

Preparing learners for the meetings

To ensure you have an interesting and lively debate, you must make it clear before the meeting (particularly before the very first simulation you use with the class) what exactly is expected of the participants. Remember that some of your students may have no experience of meetings, and that there are many different 'meeting cultures'. Here are the golden rules which will make these simulations a success:

- everyone must join in; they all have points to make and arguments to put forward

- the meeting has a clear objective: there is an issue to be addressed and, if possible, decided on – it is not enough to just talk round it

- the issue must be argued through: it is not sufficient for each participant to simply state their point of view and then contribute nothing else

- everyone must listen, take account of what others say, and be prepared to change their minds or compromise in order to reach a decision

Dos and don'ts

Before the meeting:

DO
- encourage the chairperson to get everyone to participate

- underline the importance of keeping to the point and answering the questions

- stress that more importance should be attached to what is being said than to how it is being said

- tell learners to respect the facts and arguments in their roles

During the meeting:

DO
- take a back seat if you can and intervene as little as possible

DON'T
- intervene more than you really have to

- correct language mistakes during the debate

- take a role yourself unless you have to make up numbers

Choosing students for the roles

The Managing Director/President/CEO always chairs the meeting and has the most important role. So you need someone who can really chair the meeting well, get everyone to join in, ensure they respect the rules and the facts, and conclude the meeting appropriately. As far as possible, try to change the student playing the chairperson for each meeting/situation, so that all students have a turn at this role. You will also find that there are similar job roles in the different situations, e.g. there is usually a personnel or marketing manager in most of the situations; in this case, try to vary the roles the students are given and so avoid one student having the same job in two different debates.

The main rule here is: change around as much as possible, but give important roles to those capable of doing them well.

How to manage different class sizes

It is difficult to have a real debate with fewer than three people: if you have only two or three, take a role yourself. With a large group, divide the students up into smaller groups. Don't worry if you can't use all the roles because your class, or one of the groups you split the class up into, is too small. In all the simulations there are always contradictory opinions, and hence the probability of lively discussion, in roles 'A', 'B', and 'C'. So just give each learner present a role, and leave aside the role(s) later in the alphabet.

Taking feedback notes during the meeting

Listen to the discussion and take notes. It will be impossible for you to note all mistakes, so do not try: note repeated errors, inappropriate language or lack of skills. Attach particular importance to anything which makes communication difficult.

It is also important to give positive feedback, so add notably appropriate or skilful language use and gesture to your notes. If one student persistently makes a mistake which is hindering the discussion, write a correcting note just for them and slip it to them during the debate.

Things to look out for:

Language skills	Meetings skills
vocabulary	chairing the meeting
grammar	answering the questions
appropriacy	keeping to the point
accent	participation
intonation	gesture, body language,
comprehension	expression

The use of a cassette recorder

It can be useful to record the discussion, or parts of it. This will enable you, out of class and before the next lesson, to do some of the feedback analysis work suggested above in 'Taking feedback notes during the meeting'. You will also have the added advantage of being able to illustrate your feedback in class with extracts from the tape, helping the students to recognize their own strong and weak points. Avoid playing the entire discussion with your learners, as this would quickly become very tedious.

The use of video

It is an excellent idea to film parts of the discussion if you can, because you will later be able to use the film to illustrate strong and weak points of all aspects of students' performance during the meeting. An ideal way to use the film is to show relevant extracts from the discussion to the students and ask them to:

- comment on the quality of the debate and on their own contribution (positive as well as negative points)

- correct themselves and others

- suggest ways they could have improved their communication – language, intonation, gesture, expression, body language

Avoid showing the whole film, as this could get very tedious. Try also not to do all of the comments, correction and suggestions yourself; these can be much more beneficial if done by the students themselves.

Before filming, make it clear to the students that you are doing it for follow-up work; they should not feel they are debating for the camera. You might have students who are reluctant or who refuse to be filmed; try to persuade them of the usefulness of filming, but don't go ahead if they really can't be convinced. Alternatively, you could try just filming a small part of the debate at first, to get them used to having a video camera around.

Learner follow-up and evaluation

It will help learners considerably with language and communication skills, as well as helping with the quality of later debates, if you have a phase of follow-up and evaluation after the discussion. This can be included in the video section if you film the learners.

If you have had several discussion groups because you have a large class, it will be interesting for the whole class to discuss and compare the conclusions reached by these groups. If the conclusions are different, they should try to find out why, and be prepared to explain and defend their decisions.

Photocopy and hand out the evaluation sheet to the learners, and give them time to read through and answer the questions, so they can assess their own participation in the simulation. They can then discuss their evaluation, perhaps in pairs or small groups before talking together as a class. Be careful not to turn this phase into a 'trial' of those who did not participate fully, or who failed to make themselves understood. However, criticism from fellow students is often easier to accept and more fruitful, than from the teacher.

The ideal outcome is for learners to analyse and evaluate themselves; the next best thing is for them to analyse and evaluate each other. Only if you can get them to do neither of these should you use your notes or the video film to make comments yourself. When you do this, never criticize individuals: point out where a mistake was made, and encourage the class to correct it.

If you get little response from your learners to the questions below, use the list of categories in the section on 'Taking feedback notes' to bring up different points. Do not go right through your list. Pick out those items which seemed to make the meeting less successful, and which will help to make the next meeting better.

Remember that this follow-up and evaluation is extremely helpful in improving confidence and accuracy, but is not central to *Business Roles'* main aim of developing fluency, done through active participation in the discussions. If the students are still engaged in fruitful and useful discussion ten minutes before the class ends, and are engrossed in their roles and getting their points across, don't stop the meeting to do the follow-up – let them carry on.

Evaluation sheet

Was I well prepared for the meeting?	
Did I contribute to the outcome of the debate?	
Did I participate sufficiently?	
Did I talk too much?	
Was I successful in convincing the others with my arguments?	
Was it clear what I meant when I spoke?	
Did I understand what was said? If not, why not?	
Was it a good discussion? Why/Why not?	
Did I listen carefully to the others and take account of what they said? Did I change my mind in the face of convincing arguments?	
Could I have improved my vocabulary, accent or intonation?	
Could I have improved my other communication skills?	
Did the meeting go the way I expected? Why/Why not?	

Business Roles
Evaluation sheet

© Cambridge
University Press
1997

The magazine

Introduction

You are in charge of the in-house magazine in your company. What do you do in these situations?

1. The president calls you into his office and asks why his photo was not on the cover of the last magazine published. Do you:

   a) politely explain that people in the firm are fed up with seeing his photo?
   b) promise to put his photo on the next publication?
   c) explain that it was a mistake?
   d) offer your resignation?

2. The financial manager tells you your magazine is much too expensive. Do you:

   a) try to justify the cost?
   b) tell her she must speak to the president about it?
   c) promise to try to reduce costs?
   d) tell her it's none of her business?

3. You sent out a questionnaire asking readers to say what they think of the magazine. Only 50 are sent back (out of 3,000). Do you:

   a) continue as before?
   b) radically change the contents and format of the magazine?
   c) lie about the number of questionnaires returned?
   d) send out another questionnaire?

4. Several people admit they never even open the magazine when they get it. Do you:

   a) decide to make it glossier and more attractive?
   b) change the editorial committee?
   c) give the names of these people to the president?
   d) take sick leave?

5. The Information Technology Manager suggests replacing the magazine with a weekly newsheet, sent by electronic mail to employees' offices. Do you:

   a) publish an article explaining the dangers of using electronic mail?
   b) say you will put the I.T. Manager's photo on the next magazine cover if he drops his proposal?
   c) publish a compromising picture of the I.T. Manager?
   d) do nothing, as you know your magazine can fight off attacks on every front?

6. You have had complaints about news being out of date when published. Do you:

   a) try to speed up publication?
   b) publish every two months instead of every three?
   c) write only ageless articles?
   d) blame the Post Office?

Photocopiable

Business Roles
The Magazine

© Cambridge
University Press
1997

The magazine

Situation

You work for the Layetana Beef Company, whose head office is in Rosario, Argentina. You produce, process, export and market beef all over the world, but your main markets are in North America, Europe, and the Far East. All your marketing and sales is done by fully-owned subsidiaries in the different countries, and English is the common language for your employees.

With a worldwide organization of this sort, efficient internal communication, in particular between head office in Argentina and the subsidiaries, is vital. You use the usual means for this communication – telephone, fax and e-mail. On a daily basis, this works well, but employees around the world have complained that while they get the day-to-day information they need to do business, they are not well-informed of what is happening in the company in general.

An attempt was made last year to solve this problem by publishing an in-house magazine. Every employee, everywhere in the world, receives at their home a copy of this magazine every three months. It is in colour, has lots of photos, and contains an editorial from the president, information about company strategy and business, and news from head office and the subsidiaries. As more employees speak Spanish or English than any other languages (see pie-chart), articles in the magazine are in Spanish, with a summary in English next to them, or in English, with a summary in Spanish.

You are meeting today to review company policy on internal communication.

You must decide:

- why employees still complain about a lack of information within the company

- what could be done to solve the problem

- whether the magazine is useful in its present form or whether it should be modified or replaced

---

Business Roles
The Magazine

© Cambridge
University Press
1997

Fact sheet

Location of Layetana's employees globally

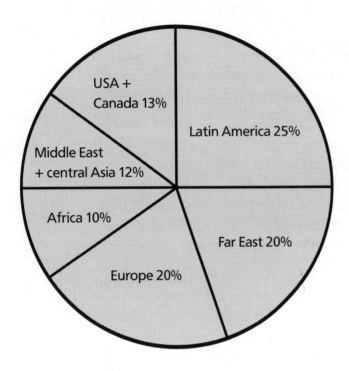

Languages spoken by Layetana's employees

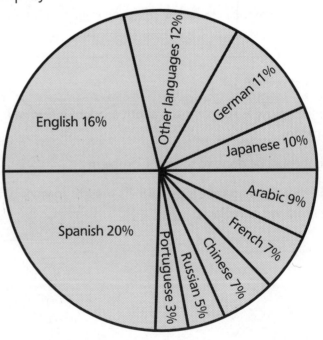

Business Roles
The Magazine

© Cambridge
University Press
1997

a

Role: **The President**

Chairing the meeting: You chair the meeting, make sure everyone participates, and ensure that decisions are made today. Organize the meeting in the following way:

Ask each participant for their opinions and list on the board:

• communication problems within the company worldwide

• proposed solutions for these problems

• problems with the magazine

• if you continue publication of the magazine, ways of improving it

Your own point of view: You are delighted with the magazine as it is today, and see no reason to change it. It is very glossy and colourful, and has always greatly interested the workforce. The strong points are, of course, your photo (which you've managed to get onto the front cover in four out of the five issues published so far), and 'The President Speaks' – your editorial, or 'leader' as you prefer to call it, on the inside cover.

Business Roles
The Magazine

© Cambridge
University Press
1997

---

b

Role: **The Head of Information Technology**

You are convinced that nobody ever reads the magazine. This does not surprise you. There isn't much real news in it, and the articles are out of date by the time it reaches the readers. It's a very good publicity brochure for the company, but that's not what it's published for.

You agree that there is a problem of communication with the subsidiaries. Employees worldwide need to be better informed of things like new appointments, who the different managers are in head office and in the subsidiaries, and new products or sales campaigns.

You think the magazine should be scrapped, and replaced by a weekly page of news on appointments, sales and products, to be sent by e-mail to all employees who have a computer in their office. This would be inexpensive, easy to manage, quick, and efficient. The articles would be short and to the point, and the news would be up-to-date. It could easily be stored for future reference. It would no longer be necessary to send articles in two languages. They could be sent in Spanish or English, whichever was more appropriate for the employee concerned.

Business Roles
The Magazine

© Cambridge
University Press
1997

Role: **The Personnel Manager, Frankfurt**

C You are the only person present who really knows about communication problems with head office. Your colleagues in Frankfurt have no problem getting sales figures and product information, but they want and need much more information about who does what in the company, and how the different subsidiaries work. The magazine has created a certain sense of unity and belonging in the company, but its content is much too head office-centred, and there's too much about strategy and management, and not enough about other countries and ordinary workers. You resent the fact that the magazine is only in Spanish and English. As the pie charts show, only a minority of employees speak these languages.

You would prefer a much less glossy publication, with more real news, and articles in simple language about the everyday lives of ordinary employees. At least a page per magazine should be in the local language, or at least in another international language like German or French. And could you please have all those photos of the President removed?

Role: **The Communications Manager**

d You don't really understand why there are complaints about communication. All vital information is communicated by phone, fax or e-mail, and background information about the structure and policy of the company, and appointments and employees around the world, is published in the magazine.

The best way to improve the magazine would be to remove the President's photo from the front cover, and to get articles about the workers inside, instead of news of company strategy and production methods. But mind what you say! Your next pay rise might depend on what you say to the President about this.

Role: **The Financial Controller**

e You think that internal communication is just a passing fashion that your company doesn't need – and it's an expensive fashion. Your glossy magazine is very attractive, but much too costly to produce and distribute; it gives no positive results, except for compliments from people outside the company who aren't even supposed to read it.

Those people in the company who need to communicate, do so. Generally people don't need to communicate with their colleagues in other departments and other countries, and they just get on with their job perfectly efficiently.

If anyone can convince you of the need for written communication between head office and overseas subsidiaries, you might agree with the idea of a simple typewritten newsletter. The best thing to do with the people from the communication department would be to fire them and so save the money wasted on their inflated salaries.

Role: **The Marketing Manager**

You have more contact than anyone else in the company with fellow managers and employees around the world. You feel that not enough is done to bring everyone together, to give them a feeling of belonging to a family, or to create a corporate identity. People need to know what is going on, who does what and where, who has been appointed to this or that post, and so on. Information in the magazine is already out of date before it is published. What you need instead is something much simpler, less glossy and more informative.

You also think company news played on video screens in the entrance hall or the staff restaurant would be useful, and you support the idea of sending news by e-mail.

Role: **The Director of Human Resources**

You feel the magazine has been a great success, but would like to make one significant change to help it to really reach all employees:

At the moment the magazine is published in Spanish and English; this is fine for staff in other countries who can speak and read English well, but it's no use for employees in the same countries who can't and who can only look at the pictures. You would therefore suggest publishing the magazine in several different languages – how about Spanish, English, Japanese and German? Maybe later you could also publish in French and Arabic.

Role: **Assistant to the Communications Manager**

You are proud of your magazine, for which you write articles and take photos. You sent out a questionnaire after the first two issues, and got very positive replies: 65% of readers said they read most of the articles, and only 3% said they only looked at the photos – although it's true that of 3,000 employees worldwide only about 500 sent back the questionnaire.

You are in favour of improving internal communication. This could be done partly by giving more practical information in the magazine (rather than talking all the time about the President and about company strategy), and partly by publishing an additional monthly or even fortnightly 'newsflash', to give up-to-the-minute news of new appointments, orders or products.

The magazine

In brief
An Argentine beef exporter looks at problems of internal communication worldwide. The glossy in-house magazine comes in for particular scrutiny.

Structure and procedure of the simulation

Introduction *(optional)* – 10-15 minutes

Preparation – 15-20 minutes

Simulation – 30-60 minutes

Follow-up *(optional)* – 15-20 minutes

Introduction
This takes the form of a questionnaire. It is light-hearted, but is designed to point out some of the problems involved in publishing an in-house magazine, to encourage discussion, and to pave the way for the simulation.

In pairs, ask the learners to discuss and make their choices. Then ask them to explain their choices to the whole class; discussion should ensue.

Preparation
See 'General notes for teachers', p 2, for details on preparing learners for the simulation.

Simulation
See 'General notes for teachers', p 2, for details on managing the simulation.

Follow-up
See 'General notes for teachers', p 2, for details on feedback techniques and evaluation.

Summary of story

The Layetana Beef Company has had complaints from employees that internal communication of information about the company, the subsidiaries and employees around the world is not good. Only last year a glossy in-house magazine was launched as a response to this problem, but not everyone is satisfied with the magazine. Today, managers are meeting to discuss the problem, and to decide if the magazine should be replaced by other means of communication, or improved. Other means of communication suggested are a video screen with company news, a page of news sent by e-mail, and a fortnightly newsflash. Complaints about the magazine concern its 'head office orientation', the excessive number of photos of the president, the president's editorial, and the publication in only two languages, Spanish and English.

Business background

A useful distinction to make in the area of internal communication is between what you might call 'functional' or 'everyday' communication on the one hand, and 'organized' or 'structured' communication on the other. Internal communication of the first sort must and does take place by phone, mail, fax, telex, e-mail, memos, and face-to-face. The second, 'organized' type of communication might take the form of a magazine, a newsletter, an e-mail information page, video cassettes (on permanent display or sent out to branches and subsidiaries), or presentations.

Internal communication of the organized structured sort is controversial. Perhaps the two extremes of opinion are:

'Accessible, organized, user-friendly and regular communication is vital to the survival of the company, to employee motivation and to the corporate culture' and
'Internal communication is a waste of time and money. Nobody knows what the people in communication do.'

It is suggested (by some in this simulation, for example) that a nice in-house magazine can in fact be used more for external communication. This is frequently the case in big firms, and is an argument to justify expenditure on a glossy publication.

Outline of roles

A: The President: is very happy with his (or her) glossy magazine.

B: Head of I.T.: thinks magazine is a waste of time and money; suggests weekly newspage on e-mail instead.

C: Personnel Manager, Frankfurt: sees a need for improvement of organized internal communication worldwide; thinks employees want more information about employees and subsidiaries, and that magazine is too head office-oriented ; suggests a page in German or French.

D: Communications Manager: is satisfied that magazine meets company's needs for internal communication, but wants to get the president's photo out, and news about the workers in.

E: Financial Controller: thinks magazine is too costly; sees no need for organized communication.

F: Marketing Manager: wants something more up-to-date and informative than the present magazine; proposes video news in entrance hall.

G: Director of Human Resources: wants magazine published in several different languages.

H: Assistant to Communications Manager: proud of magazine; points out that only 3% admit to looking only at the photos; suggests fortnightly 'newsflash' in addition.

Possible outcome

This will probably be a very open discussion, and there are several seemingly sound solutions. The magazine is certain to be criticized, and it is very likely that the participants will decide to make changes to it; the president's photo will probably be cut from the magazine, topics will be made more employee-centred and one or two more languages will be used for the main articles.

It is quite likely that the magazine will be kept, though, and that other suggestions (the strongest candidate possibly being the e-mail newspage) will be adopted to use alongside it.

Vocabulary

appointment: (here) selection of new member of staff

fed up: annoyed by something you have experienced for too long

a compromising photo: a photo of someone in an embarrassing situation that could be used against them, e.g. the president asleep at their desk, or handcuffed to a police officer

costly: expensive

editor: person in charge of a publication

editorial: article in a publication, written by the editor to express their opinion (but here written by the president)

efficient: effective, works well

electronic mail (e-mail): a system for sending and leaving messages by computer

to fire: to dismiss from a job

fully-owned subsidiary: a company whose shares are all owned by its parent company

glossy: bright, shiny

in-house magazine: company publication, produced for employees only

inflated: too high

internal communication: any communication between employees of the same company

modified: changed

out of date: old

overseas: in other countries

to resent: dislike, take exception to

to scrap: abandon, give up

up-to-the-minute news: the very latest news

The training budget

Introduction

1. What sorts of training does your company (or a company you have worked in) offer?

2. Does the company spend a lot of money on training?

3. Why is priority given to some training courses rather than others?

4. Is the training always useful? Do people do it because they really need it for their work or because they just find it interesting?

Business Roles
The Training Budget

© Cambridge
University Press
1997

The training budget

Situation

You work for Ipswich Union, a large insurance company with its head office in Ipswich, a town in the east of England. Of the 400 employees at head office, over half work in the claims department and nearly 100 work in sales and marketing. The other departments are much smaller: the personnel department and the finance department each employ about 30 people, and the communications department and the international department each employ about 20 people.

The main activity in an insurance company is of course to sell policies, and then to deal with claims. This is why three-quarters of the staff at Ipswich Union are involved in these activities. Your company recently installed a new computer network in your offices: every employee has a micro-computer on their desk, and all the processes of drawing up policies and dealing with claims are computerized. All the departments can use the network for their type of work (accounting, billing, payslips, etc.) and everyone has access to the electronic mail system.

Because many of your customers travel abroad, you have more and more contact with foreign countries, particularly in Europe. In addition, your company has decided to expand its activities into Europe and has recently signed agreements with a German and an Italian firm, who are going to market your health and life insurance policies in their countries. The company is hoping to sign similar agreements with firms in several other European countries.

You are meeting today to discuss the training budget for next year. The company spends a generous 5-6% of turnover on training. Most managers agree that this is generous but necessary; where you have more difficulty agreeing is how to share out this budget. You each have a list showing how the budget was allocated for this year's training.

You must decide:

• whether money allocated for training this year has been well spent

• what training should be done next year

• if any new courses should be added to the list

• how many people in each department should benefit from each training course

• what percentage of the budget should be spent on each item

Business Roles
The Training Budget

© Cambridge
University Press
1997

Fact sheet

Course	This year		Next year	
	no. of participants	% of budget	no. of participants	% of budget
computers (handling policies and claims)	45	19		
languages (French, Spanish, Italian, German)	22	17		
sales techniques	25	15		
public relations	15	10		
telephone manners	15	10		
accounting, financial management	7	10		
using e-mail	20	9		
personnel management (pay, recruitment)	5	6		
aesthetics (flower arranging)	1	2		
physical development (tennis lessons)	2	2		

New types of training for next year

....

....

....

Business Roles
The Training Budget

© Cambridge
University Press
1997

a

Role: **The Chief Executive**

Chairing the meeting: You chair the meeting, and ensure everyone participates. Organize the meeting in the following way:

1. Listen carefully to what each head of department has to say. They must explain why and how the money has been spent on the different sorts of training this year, and how many members of staff did each course. Each manager must also say how they would like the budget to be spent next year.

2. Get agreement on the percentage of the budget to be allocated to each type of training. Write the percentages up on the board.

Your own point of view: You personally asked for just one course this year. Your secretary did a flower arranging course so they could make attractive flower arrangements for your office, the boardroom, and the entrance hall. They have done very well, and won't need any more lessons. For the coming year, you would like to see more training in the use of the e-mail, which was an expensive investment but is under-used. And you think more members of staff should learn European languages to facilitate your expansion into the European market, which is your main ambition for the company.

Business Roles
The Training Budget

© Cambridge University Press 1997

---

b

Role: **The Marketing Manager**

You think the company spends too much on languages. It is true that you are expanding into Europe, but this is being done in partnership with European firms who handle all the business in their countries. When they do need to communicate with you, their English is quite good enough.

The whole future of your company is dependent on sales and marketing – on finding customers and keeping them. You are convinced that at least half of the training budget should be spent on training and motivating sales and marketing staff, together with the people in communication and advertising – provided they are directly involved in the sales effort. Only 20 of your staff of nearly 100 have done training in sales techniques this year: this is quite inadequate.

The item called 'physical development' in this year's plan is, in fact, tennis lessons, which you took on the company's indoor court with your sales manager. You think tennis lessons (or it could be squash or golf) are an excellent way of motivating your staff, and would like to see this possibility extended to others.

Business Roles
The Training Budget

© Cambridge University Press 1997

Role: **The Claims Manager**

C You have a very important role in the company. Your department has more staff than any other – in fact half the head office staff work under you.

You welcomed the decision to put a PC on every desk, and this has immensely increased efficiency and speeded up handling of claims. Unfortunately, your staff have not had enough training in how to use the computers. It is ridiculous to spend money on flower arrangements, tennis, public relations and telephone manners, when most of your staff have had no training in handling claims by computer. Only 25 of your 200 staff have had this training this year.

For the coming year, you need no fewer than 100 staff to be trained in handling claims by computer. With the increasing internationalization of the company, you need a few of your staff to begin or continue studying European languages, especially French and Spanish.

Business Roles
The Training Budget

© Cambridge
University Press
1997

Role: **The Communications Manager**

d You personally recommended the installation of e-mail when the computer network was installed. You are disappointed that this means of communication is under-used and think that it is because staff (in all departments) need training in using it. Only 20 people in the whole company have done a course this year, and this must be made the number one priority for next year's training.

You also recommended the public relations and telephone manners courses this year. These were very useful for the 30 members of staff who had them (you chose those who were in most constant touch with the public), but you would like another 20 people – 10 for the phone, 10 for public relations – to do the course now.

Business Roles
The Training Budget

© Cambridge
University Press
1997

Role: **Head of the International Department**

Your staff have more and more frequent contact with foreign countries. Those handling claims need Spanish and French in particular, and those responsible for contacts with your European partners need Italian and German. You feel you must allocate more money to language training: it is simply not true that everyone in Europe speaks English, and it is not polite, and does not make business sense, to assume that your partners are ready to speak to you in English on every occasion. Only 12 of your 20 staff have done language courses this year: you would like all 20 to have them next year. You also suggest that more people in the other departments do language lessons, especially those in communication and marketing.

Role: **The Personnel Manager**

You think that extra spending on using computers for claims, policies, or the e-mail could not be justified. All the claims staff already use their computers for handling claims: most of them have had no training and they manage perfectly well. The same is true for staff using computers to draw up policies. The e-mail is simple to use: training staff to use it is a waste of time and money. It is true that not many people do use it, but this is because staff prefer using other means of communication, like the telephone or memos.

What you would really like is for your own staff to do more of the training they started this year. What could be more important than an efficient pay department? Everyone wants to get paid at the end of the month, and to have no mistakes on their payslip. You agree your department is small, but 6% on training for such an essential service is very little.

Role: **The Financial Manager**

Unlike your colleagues, you think that spending on training is too high. You want to persuade them to reduce the overall figure to 5%. In your opinion, money is being wasted – tennis and flower arrangement courses should be stopped; public relations and telephone manners are just fashions and training for them is not useful; too much is being spent on languages, given the small number of people who need them.

You want to concentrate the training budget on accounting, financial management, and handling claims and policies by computer.

The training budget

In brief
What percentage of the training budget should the Ipswich Union, a major insurance company based in Ipswich in the east of England, spend on each item in the coming year? Should you spend more on sales and marketing techniques (vital for new business) or on training claims staff (the heart of the business)? Can you justify spending on language classes or e-mail? How vital are public relations and phone manners?

Structure and procedure of the simulation

Introduction *(optional)* – 20-30 minutes

Preparation – 15-20 minutes

Simulation – 45-60 minutes

Follow-up *(optional)* – 15-20 minutes

Introduction
Discuss the questions as a group, or divide a large class into smaller groups. The aim is to get learners to give as many ideas as possible of the different types of training which might be available in their jobs. List answers on the board.

Possible answers: languages, computers (this could cover a lot of different types of courses), accounting, financial control, creativity, communication (this too could cover a lot of things from public relations through journalism to advertising), typing, marketing, sales techniques, engineering, electronics. You may well get answers concerning very specific skills.

Explore whether the learners' employers spend a lot or little on training, whether this is important, what sort of companies spend a lot and why. And try to discover if there is a distinction between necessary training on the one hand and just useful and interesting on the other.

Preparation
See the section 'General notes for teachers', p 2, for details on preparing learners for the simulation.

The reference sheet gives numbers of employees who did each kind of course this year, with the percentage of the budget spent on each item. Participants can fill in the numbers and percentages for the coming year as they decide on them. There is space at the bottom of the sheet for any new items which might be added for the coming year.

Simulation
See the section 'General notes for teachers', p 2, for details on managing the simulation.

Note: Agreement on percentages for next year's training budget are the aim for the <u>end</u> of the meeting. There should first be debate about what training is most important to the company and the direction it is going, as the roles are designed to produce disagreement on this point and so discussion.

Follow-up
See the section 'General notes for teachers', p 2, for details on feedback techniques and evaluation.

Summary of story

Management at the Ipswich Union insurance company are meeting to decide on what percentage of the training budget, which is a generous 5-6% of turnover, should be spent on each type of course next year. At the moment, the largest share goes on computer courses, language training and sales techniques training. This is quite logical: there is now a computer on every desk, and staff need to know how to use them; there are many claims from continental Europe, so staff need to be able to speak a variety of foreign languages; and of course every company needs to be able to sell successfully. However, the managers present all have strong opinions on how the money should be spent next year, and initially seem set to disagree.

Business background

Training is vital to the future of practically every company, big or small. Different companies will, of course, have different needs: in manufacturing the accent will be on technology, whereas in services it will be on marketing, sales and communication. In recent years a lot of training time has been devoted to communication, creativity and total quality.

Ipswich Union spends a lot of money on training (5-6% of turnover); most companies spend much less.

The ideal organization of training may be: the training manager discusses training needs with each department head, makes a plan, sets up the courses (inside or, very often, outside the company) and then assesses results. In practice there may be no training manager (training is looked after by the personnel manager); there is no training plan, and each department decides for itself what it needs.

Outline of roles

A: Chief Executive: is ready to end aesthetics course, but wants more training in e-mail and in languages.

B: Marketing Manager: thinks too much is spent on languages and not enough on sales techniques.

C: Claims Manager: wants more staff to have training in handling claims by computer.

D: Communications Manager: wants more training to use the e-mail, and for some people to do public relations and telephone manners courses.

E: Head of International Department: wants all 20 people in their department to do language training.

F: Personnel Manager: wants more training in personnel management.

G: Financial Manager: wants to reduce overall spending on training, and to concentrate on accounting, financial management, and handling claims by computer.

Possible outcome

This is very difficult to predict, except that aesthetics will certainly be dropped, and physical development will probably not be retained. If the marketing manager is good, he or she might well persuade the meeting to spend less on languages and more on sales and marketing. The claims manager also has pretty strong arguments for computer courses. The electronic mail might come in for a hard time. But this will probably be a very open debate, and most courses will probably be retained with small changes to the percentages.

Vocabulary

accounting: the system of recording and classifying business and financial transactions

claims: demands by customers of an insurance firm for reimbursement following an accident or loss

computer network: a group of computers and terminals linked for the sharing of data

electronic mail (e-mail): a system for sending and leaving messages by computer

insurance: financial protection against risk, loss or ruin

payslip: document showing weekly or monthly wage received and any deductions, e.g. for income tax

policy: in insurance terms, this is the contract insurance companies sign with their customers

training: education, improvement of skills and knowledge

turnover: total business done by a company in a given period

Changing names

Introduction

1. **With a partner, think of and write down the names and brands of a few well-known companies which:**

a) have the same name for the company and its products.

....

....

b) have one name for the company and another or others for its products.

....

....

c) have one name for the company, use the company name for some products and other names for other products.

....

....

Now discuss and note down reasons why you think these companies have such policies for brand names.

2. **Once you have done this, discuss as a group:**

a) Do some companies have too many brand names?

b) Why do some companies create new brand names or change their company or brand name?

c) What are the advantages and disadvantages of having the *same* name for the company and the products?

d) What are the advantages and disadvantages of having *different* names for the company and the products, and of having a range of brand names?

Business Roles
Changing names

© Cambridge
University Press
1997

Changing names

Situation

You work for Compagnia Europea di Biciclette, the biggest bicycle manufacturer in Europe. You have factories in Bologna and Siena in Italy, at Evreux in France, and at Cambridge in England. The head office is in Siena, Italy. You have six different brand names – *Bicibolo, Pedalissimo, Bachtung, Evélo, Rose* and *Wheeler.*

You are meeting today to discuss both the group name and the brand names. It has been suggested that your group name is unsuitable for the following reasons:

– it's Italian, so not really suitable for the European market leader
– it's too long and too difficult to say
– awareness of the name is poor

**Compagnia Europea
di Biciclette**

Some of your managers think the group has too many brand names. They argue that as the products are much the same whichever factory they are made in, sales would improve if you could concentrate advertising and marketing effort and budgets on fewer brands. The reason you have so many brand names is that when the different subsidiaries manufacturing bicycles and using their own brand names were taken over by Compagnia Europea di Biciclette, these names were kept. Different brands of bicycle are strong in the markets of different European countries, but at least three of your brands are available nearly everywhere.

You must decide:

• if the group needs a new corporate name

• if you should keep all the brand names

• if you could use the same name for the corporation and for a brand

Business Roles
Changing names

© Cambridge
University Press
1997

Compagnia Europea di Biciclette

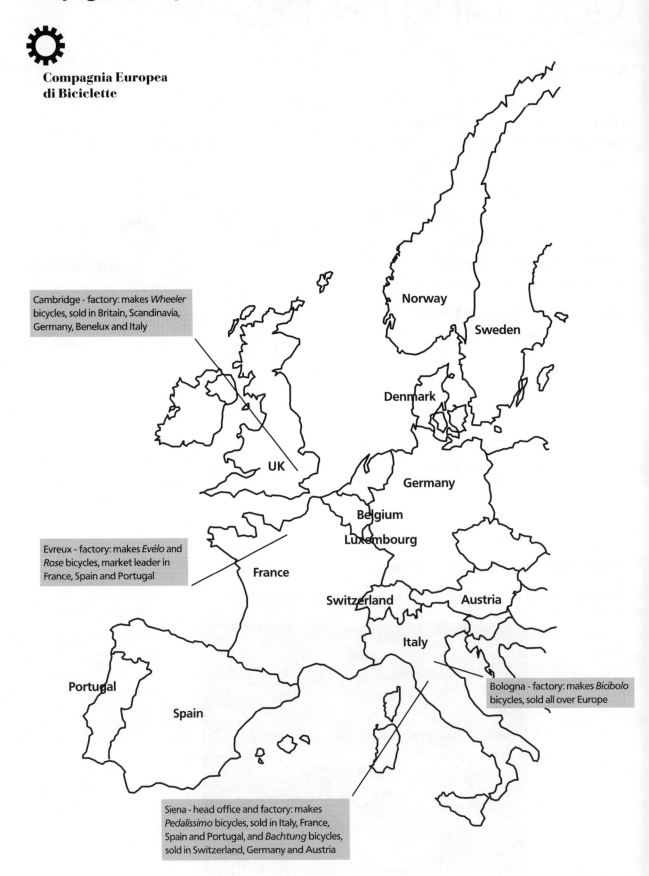

**Compagnia Europea
di Biciclette**

Cambridge - factory: makes *Wheeler* bicycles, sold in Britain, Scandinavia, Germany, Benelux and Italy

Evreux - factory: makes *Evélo* and *Rose* bicycles, market leader in France, Spain and Portugal

Bologna - factory: makes *Bicibolo* bicycles, sold all over Europe

Siena - head office and factory: makes *Pedalissimo* bicycles, sold in Italy, France, Spain and Portugal, and *Bachtung* bicycles, sold in Switzerland, Germany and Austria

Norway

Sweden

Denmark

UK

Germany

Belgium

Luxembourg

France

Switzerland

Austria

Italy

Portugal

Spain

Business Roles
Changing names

© Cambridge
University Press
1997

Role: **The Managing Director**

a

Chairing the meeting: Make sure everyone speaks and gives their point of view. Listen to what they all have to say, and try to come to a collective decision; if you cannot, make the decision yourself. Organize the meeting in the following way, writing key information on the board as the meeting progresses:

1. Get opinions on whether the group needs a new name, and if so, what it should be.

2. Discuss whether the company has too many brand names; if it does, which ones should be dropped?

3. Discuss whether the same name could be used for both the group and for the products. What name should you choose?

Your own point of view: When you ask people what sort of bike they own, they frequently say it's a *Wheeler* or a *Bicibolo*. But you find it very annoying that few people seem to have heard of your corporate name. You don't really mind what name is adopted for the company or the products, but want something which can quickly become well-known.

Role: **The Plant Manager, Cambridge**

You are the manager of the Cambridge plant, which makes *Wheeler* bicycles. You were taken over by Compagnia Europea di Biciclette in 1986. You were relieved that you did not have to take the brand name *Bicibolo* for either your subsidiary or your products after the takeover, because you believe that your factory has much higher standards of quality than the Italian factories and that the *Bicibolo* bicycle is an inferior product.

You agree that the group could do with fewer brand names, but think that *Wheeler* is obviously an excellent name for a bike and should be kept. You are not sure the group needs to change its corporate name, but if it does it could take the name 'Wheeler' – provided the other factories made an effort to raise their quality to the same standard as yours.

Role: **The Marketing Manager**

C You wouldn't mind changing the firm's name, but are definitely against any idea of either using a brand name as the firm's name, or dropping any of the brand names used at the moment. Your reasons are:

- you know that if you take one of the better-known brand names as the firm's name, the dealers selling the other brands, and the factories making them, will be offended

- by having different names and ranges you keep a hold on the market, and keep competitors out. In most Italian cities you have three different outlets for *Pedalissimo*, *Bicibolo* and *Wheeler*, and if you used just one of those names, you might well lose the two other dealers

---

Role: **The Communications Manager**

d You want a new company name which will be easy for everyone to remember, and which will help to create a group culture. Your suggestion is 'Eurocycles'.

You are not against having two or three trade names, but think six is ridiculous. *Bicibolo* seems to you a good name, is by far the best known in Italy, and has a good reputation in Europe. *Rose* is a ridiculous name for a bicycle, and *Wheeler* rather wet. *Evélo* has a good reputation in southern Europe, and should be used alongside *Bicibolo*. You should drop *Pedalissimo*, which you find silly, and *Bachtung*, which is much too German-sounding for a bike which is not at all made in German-speaking countries.

Remind your colleagues that the *Bicibolo* team won the Tour de France last year. The billion lira it cost did much, in your opinion, to give the brand name *Bicibolo* a sound European reputation.

Role: **The Personnel Manager**

f You work at the head office in Siena. You want to create some sort of corporate identity and group culture which would help to bring the different subsidiaries together, and make your employees proud of working for the group.

It is obvious that the starting point for all this must be the name of the group and the names of the products. Nobody has ever heard of Compagnia Europea di Biciclette, so a new name (why not 'Eurocycles'?) would be an excellent idea.

As long as you have each factory making its own brand, you will have damaging rivalry between each subsidiary. You should get rid of some brand names straight away, and gradually phase in a common name. Why not use the same name as the group, namely *Eurocycles*?

Role: **The Production Manager**

You know only too well that any change in the company's name or the brand names would create terrible problems in the factories.

The corporate name: When the French and English factories were taken over, they were worried that they might have to adopt one of the Italian brand names as a corporate name; 'Compagnia Europea di Biciclette' was much easier to accept. Your colleagues must remember that although the factories are all part of one group now, before the takeovers ten years or more ago, they all used to compete against each other.

Brand names: All the brand names are closely associated with a factory. So at Evreux, they are proud of their *Evélos*, and are convinced they are the best bikes in the business. At Cambridge they are just as proud of their *Wheelers*, at Siena of their *Pedalissimos* and at Bologna of their *Bicibolos*. *Rose* is used as a name for girls' bikes, and *Bachtung* is an excellent name for marketing in Germanic countries.

Business Roles
Changing names

© Cambridge
University Press
1997

Role: **The Financial Controller**

You are against any costly changes. You agree that the group is not well-known, and that you do have rather a lot of brand names. But you are worried about the cost of changing the group's name – think of all that wasted notepaper, and the cost of a corporate advertising campaign. Perhaps there might be savings to be made if you only had one or two brand names. After all, what a lot of money was wasted by having six different stands at the Frankfurt Show last year!

Listen to what your colleagues have to say, and try to persuade them to choose the least costly solution. Tell them also that you want more back on your money than you got from last year's Tour de France. The *Bicibolo* team won, but the other sponsor, Perrier, got all the publicity!

Business Roles
Changing names

© Cambridge
University Press
1997

Role: **The Plant Manager, Evreux**

You consider your products to be the best in the group. Your makes *Evélo* and *Rose* are market leaders in France, Spain and Portugal. It would be a disaster if you scrapped these names. *Rose* may be a bit soppy, but your pink girls' range sells very well. *Evélo* helps your employees identify with the firm, as you are well-known locally.

You'd like to change the group name, as you think that it's too Italian. How about 'Eurocycles'?

Business Roles
Changing names

© Cambridge
University Press
1997

Changing names

In brief

A bicycle manufacturer, which has its head office in Italy and several factories around Europe, must decide if it needs to change its corporate name and to reduce the number of brand names it uses. If they change the corporate name, should they adopt one of their current brand names as the new corporate name? Different brands are strong in the different markets, so is there really a case for reducing the names? If there is, which ones should go and which remain?

Structure and procedure of the simulation

Introduction (optional) – 15-20 minutes

Preparation – 15-20 minutes

Simulation – 30-60 minutes

Follow-up (optional) – 15-20 minutes

Introduction

Answers

For question 1, get learners to work in pairs. Their answers will vary according to where you are and what nationality your learners are.

1. *possible answers:* a. BP, Nike, Boeing, IBM, 3M, Sony; b. General Motors (Opel, Vauxhall), Proctor and Gamble (Ariel); c. Fiat (Magneti Marelli, Solex), Volkswagen (Audi), Electrolux (Zanussi), Ford (Jaguar), Mars (M & M's), Danone (Gervais, Lu).

You will soon discover that it is hard to split the companies suggested into clear-cut categories. Ford, for example, usually uses its own name on its products, but not for the products of its subsidiary, Jaguar. The aim here is to get at the reasons behind companies choosing corporate and brand names. For question 2, work together as a class.

2a. An example here of a company with too many brand names might be the Italian car maker Fiat (Lancia, Alfa Romeo, Ferrari, Autobianchi, Fiat, Iveco). Soap powder manufacturers use several names for very similar products; Philips and Electrolux, to name just two European giants, do the same. You may not find clear-cut answers to this question, but it will be interesting (and useful for the simulation that follows) to think about why some groups have so many brand names.

b. Firms may add new brand names simply because they are bringing out a new product. It may also be because they decide to go up-market or down-market with a product very similar to one they sell already, but for marketing reasons they need to differentiate the new product from the old. Changing a corporate name to a

new one is done to create or improve corporate identity, so that employees can identify with the firm and develop a sense of belonging that leads to greater motivation and increased sales. Also, the change may seem sensible when a product name is better known than the company name. For example, a big French group called Alcatel Alsthom used to be called CGE; it chose its new name because Alcatel and Alsthom were already well-known as subsidiary and brand names. Similarly another French company, BSN, changed its corporate name to Danone, a well-known brand of yoghurt they produce.

c. Advantages: workers will be proud to say they work for your corporation if it's well-known because of the product. On the sales side, you will have more chance of having a 'brand', which customers will demand and stick to. Disadvantages: if your corporation has a problem with a product, it can get a bad name. Similarly if the corporation itself gets a bad name, because of a problem (pollution, financial irregularity), sales of its product are even more likely to suffer than if they had a different brand name.

d. Advantages: if the corporation is having problems, the public, unaware of this, will not stop buying their products. Similarly, if there are problems with the products, the corporate reputation might not be affected. With a range of brand names you can cover the entire market and so keep out competitors. A good example of this whole market coverage is the way one company will produce a large number of different soap powder brands all targeted at different sectors of the market.

Disadvantages: successful products may not be connected to the corporate name. It's possibly more difficult to create a strong image and awareness of products if you have a lot of different brand names, and budgets and marketing will have to be divided among the different brands.

Preparation

See the section 'General notes for teachers', p 2, for details on preparing learners for the simulation.

Photocopy and give out the map and fact sheet, which will show students at a glance where the factories are and which brand is manufactured in each place.

Simulation

See the section 'General notes for teachers', p 2, for details on managing the simulation.

Follow-up

See the section 'General notes for teachers', p 2, for details on feed back techniques and evaluation.

Summary of story

The biggest bike manufacturer in Europe has 'Compagnia Europea di Biciclette' as its corporate name, and six brand names. Today's meeting is to decide if it would be a good idea to change the corporate name and/or drop some of the brand names. A suggestion is also made that a new corporate name might be used as a brand name.

The group has two factories in Italy, with its head office in Siena, and factories in France and England. It may prove difficult to reduce the number of names, as each factory is attached to its own and thinks that its products are superior to the others. It will be argued that with so many brand names it is difficult to increase awareness, and hence sales, of products.

The group name is not widely known. Some will say that this doesn't matter, others that awareness of the group is important for employees and that a strong image for the corporation would help sales of the products.

Business background

The question of corporate identity, image and culture has taken on more and more importance in recent years. It goes beyond the already complex questions of the marketing and advertising of products, so much so that in some big firms, the communications manager is put in charge of this, and ranks second only to the CEO, above the marketing manager and personnel manager.

Some large groups can have a problem with corporate identity. On the positive side, if you work for Sony, you know exactly who you work for, and what the company does. Everyone has heard of the company, and knows the products. So as an employee, this is very positive, makes you proud of working for Sony, makes you want to stay and motivates you in your work.

However, this strong identity (and the distinctive work culture which certainly goes with it) may cause complications at the marketing level. Well-known makes are often up-market: their products have an image for quality and are expensive. Suppose the company wants to go down-market to increase market share. Do they then have to create a new brand name? If they do, what happens to corporate identity?

Another problem arises when a well-known group runs into financial trouble. If the brand name is the same as the group name, news of this trouble will rub off on the products, and on sales.

Outline of roles

A: Managing Director: wants a new corporate name which will quickly become well-known. Doesn't mind if the brand names are changed or not.

B: Plant Manager, Cambridge: wants fewer brand names, but insists on keeping *Wheeler*; thinks 'Wheeler ' would be good as a corporate name too.

C: Marketing Manager: wouldn't object to a new corporate name, but is against it being one of the current brand names. Is also against dropping any of the present brand names.

D: Communications Manager: likes 'Eurocycles' as a new group name. Wants to reduce the number of brand names, but thinks *Bicibolo* should definitely be kept.

E: Production Manager: is against any change: considers all brand names are very effective in their markets.

F: Personnel Manager: wants to create corporate identity by having new group name 'Eurocycles', which could also be used as a common brand name instead of the present names.

G: Financial Controller: looking for the cheapest solution.

H: Plant Manager, Evreux: defends own products' brand names – *Rose* and *Evélo*. Suggests 'Eurocycles' as the new group name.

Possible outcome

If the full number of roles is used, 'Eurocycles' is quite likely to be chosen as the new corporate name. If only a small number of roles are used, the outcome may be more open; it depends on how persuasive the Cambridge Plant Manager and the Communications Manager are about their preferred choices.

As regards the brand names, anything can happen. It is quite likely that the number of brand names will be cut down, but which names are kept will depend on how well different participants argue their cases. However, *Bachtung* and *Rose* are the weakest and so the most likely to be dropped, while *Bicibolo* would seem to be the strongest name and therefore least likely to go.

Vocabulary

to adopt: to start to use

awareness: how well-known the company, its products and its brand names are

brand name: the name on and of a company's products

corporate identity: the qualities that distinguish a company, that make people recognise it

corporate name: the name of a corporation or large group of companies

a dealer, a retailer: person who sells the product

to drop: to stop using

group culture: a way of working together, of behaving as a group

lira: the Italian currency

offended: displeased

an outlet: a shop or agency, place where products are sold

Perrier: fizzy mineral water from France, sold worldwide

rivalry: competition

soppy: silly, stupid

a subsidiary: a company owned by another company

a takeover: when one company buys another

The *Tour de France*: a world-famous bicycle race which takes place every July in France

wet: silly, not very serious

Polluting the river

Introduction

1. You are the managing director of a factory. You discover that your manufacturing process pollutes the environment. Do you:

a) try to hide the facts?
b) do everything you can to stop the pollution?
c) prepare an emergency plan for when the news leaks out?
d) invite the press to visit your 'environment-friendly' factory?

2. The news of the pollution gets out and is published in the press. Do you:

a) deny the facts?
b) admit everything?
c) cover up?
d) explain that it can't be helped?

3. The local authorities say you will be prosecuted if the pollution is not stopped immediately. Do you:

a) ask for money from them to cover the cost of changing the production process?
b) threaten to close the factory?
c) pretend to accept their orders and do nothing?
d) move to another area?

4. You agree to stop polluting, but this will add 50% to production costs. Do you:

a) ask the unions for permission to cut wages by 50%?
b) sack half the workforce?
c) increase prices by 50%?
d) save money by using cheaper parts?

5. You are fined for pollution. Do you:

a) pay the fine and carry on polluting?
b) refuse to pay because the firm will go bankrupt if you do?
c) appeal?
d) make a generous donation to the local ecology party?

6. You are sacked by the parent company because of the pollution scandal. Do you:

a) publish proof that the president knew all about the pollution before you did?
b) retire and write your memoirs?
c) apply for a job with the firm's main competitor?
d) do a university course in environmental studies?

Business Roles
Polluting the river

© Cambridge
University Press
1997

Polluting the river

Situation

Your company, Coldpoint, makes refrigerators at a factory in Bismarck, the capital city of North Dakota, USA. It is the subsidiary of a Canadian firm whose headquarters are in Hamilton, Ontario. The head office of this US subsidiary is at a modern factory in Milwaukee, Wisconsin, where the company's freezers are made. The Canadian parent firm is the market leader in North America, and your company is the number one on the US market, selling up-market refrigerators and freezers. All your products sell under the brand name 'Coldpoint', which is very well-known and has an excellent image.

The Bismarck factory was built some 33 years ago, and employs 600 of the 48,000 people living in the town. This makes it the second largest employer in the town, and a major contributor to the local economy, not least because North Dakota is sparsely populated and Bismarck is over 150 kilometres away from any other large town. Coldpoint is regarded as a reasonable employer; pay, working conditions and job security there are good.

It is common knowledge in the factory that chemical waste from the manufacturing process drains into the stream which flows through the factory site and on into the Missouri River. This has been happening for as long as the factory has been there. The pollution it causes is low-level, but the damaging effects on the stream and its animal and plant life seem to have got worse as production has increased. No complaints have been made about this, but a journalist from a local paper has now asked to visit the factory as part of a report that they are preparing on pollution in the area.

The Canadian parent company doesn't know about this problem at all, and the US managers have been very careful to keep the information from it. Fortunately for the subsidiary, Canadian policy is not to interfere with US affairs, provided business is good, but the company is very sensitive about problems of pollution.

You are meeting today to decide if your company should do anything about the pollution.

You must decide with your colleagues:

• how serious the problem is

• what, if any, action should be taken

Business Roles
Polluting the river

© Cambridge
University Press
1997

Location of Coldpoint factory and surrounding area

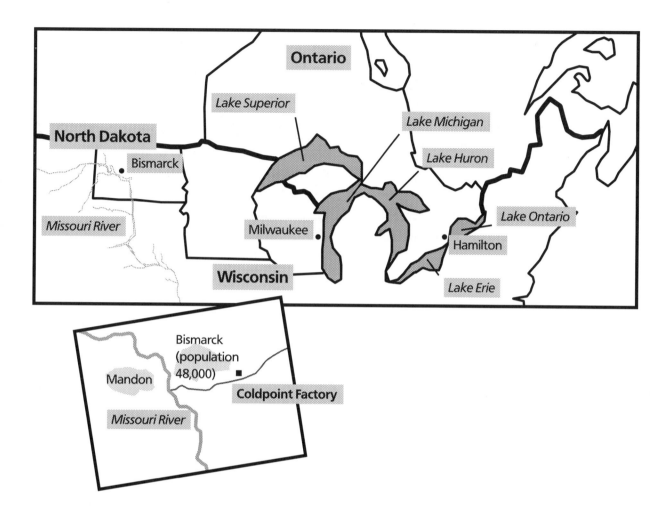

Business Roles
Polluting the river

© Cambridge
University Press
1997

Role: **The President**

a

Chairing the meeting: You are the president of the US subsidiary of Coldpoint. You have called this meeting, will chair it, and must make sure a decision is reached today. Listen to your colleagues, ensure they all give their point of view on the problem, and try to bring the discussion to a joint agreement. If there is no agreement, you yourself will have to take the final decision.

Your own point of view: Your personal opinion is that it is very risky polluting the river, and you are worried about the media publishing this information. But your usual reaction to any proposed course of action is to analyse the cost, and in general you try to concentrate on increasing productivity and on spending as little as possible, in order to maximize profits.

Find out how costly any course of action designed to put an end to the pollution might be. You also want to discover why there is a problem in Bismarck and not in Milwaukee, and the exact extent of the damage being done to the environment.

Role: **The Marketing Manager**

b

You only recently found out about this problem, and think radical action should be taken without delay. You don't know anything about the technical aspects, but as market leader in North America, and as you are dependent for sales on your excellent up-market image, you think it is essential the company avoids the certain scandal which would arise if the facts were published in the media, or became known to the county, the state, or the unions. Whatever the cost, this pollution must be stopped immediately.

Role: **The Plant Manager, Bismarck factory**

c

You have been plant manager for six years, and worked in the Bismarck plant since it was opened 33 years ago. You really can't understand what all the fuss is about. Who would be silly enough to tell the press about this problem? After all, anyone in the factory would be too worried about losing their job to say or do anything. The county and state authorities, in your opinion, already know the facts, and would rather not admit it, for fear of the factory closing down. As for the unions, they are only interested in wage rises, and you know that they know that an expensive solution to the pollution problem would mean no rises at all for several years to come. Your favourite argument is that while it's true that there are no fish in the river, there haven't been any for 33 years, so why start worrying about it now?

d

Role: **The Chemical Engineer, Bismarck plant**

You are the only person who really understands the technical aspects of the problem, which are:

About 25 tons of acid waste drains into the stream every year. This waste is an inevitable part of the manufacturing process. It kills off animal and plant life for some distance downstream.

At the Milwaukee plant, the acid is boiled away, a process which adds about 10% to production costs. Slightly toxic gas is released, but nobody seems to notice, probably because the plant is in a major industrial region. If this boiling process were to be used in Bismarck, the cost would be even greater. Because the factory in Bismarck is in a residential area, the gas would have to be filtered, adding a further 5% to production costs.

Business Roles
Polluting the river

© Cambridge University Press 1997

e

Role: **The Financial Controller**

You admit there is a problem with pollution, and are as worried as anyone about it becoming known. However, the Bismarck factory is much less profitable than the Milwaukee one, and you really don't want any new spending at the moment. You don't know anything about the technical aspects, but do know that boiling away the acid waste will add 10% to production costs, and filtering the toxic gas will add another 5%.

Productivity is 12% higher in Milwaukee than in Bismarck, admittedly because the Milwaukee factory is more modern. Costs are higher in Bismarck: it's such an out-of-the-way place that you have to pay higher salaries to attract qualified personnel, and transport costs are higher both for supplies and sales, because the factory is so far from your main markets. You think it might be better to close the Bismarck factory and transfer production to Milwaukee.

Business Roles
Polluting the river

© Cambridge University Press 1997

f

Role: **The Head of R and D**

You do your research in Milwaukee. You are concerned by the pollution in Bismarck, and agree with marketing and image arguments. However, you are worried that if action is taken in Bismarck, you might be forced to do something more to prevent air pollution in Milwaukee. After all, if, under pressure from ecologists, the local press, the unions or the county or state authorities, you started filtering the gas in Bismarck, sooner or later you'd be forced to do the same thing in Milwaukee.

Business Roles
Polluting the river

© Cambridge University Press 1997

Polluting the river

In brief

An American manufacturer of refrigerators has been draining chemical waste from its manufacturing process into the river next to its factory in Bismarck, North Dakota. Managers meet to decide what, if anything, can and should be done about this pollution.

Structure and procedure of this simulation

Introduction (optional) – 15-20 minutes

Preparation – 15-20 minutes

Simulation – 30-45 minutes

Follow-up (optional) – 15-20 minutes

Introduction

Photocopy and hand out the questionnaire to the students. It is designed to get them thinking about the topic of pollution before the simulation. When they have completed it, ask them for their answers and, more importantly, why they chose that answer. There are no 'right' answers to the questions, and you should not necessarily expect agreement among the group.

Preparation

See the section 'General notes for teachers', p 2, for details on preparing learners for the simulation.

Simulation

See the section 'General notes for teachers', p 2, for details on managing the simulation.

Follow-up

See the section 'General notes for teachers', p 2, for details on feed back techniques and evaluation.

Summary of story

Coldpoint is the American subsidiary of a Canadian manufacturer of refrigerators and freezers. It has a factory producing refrigerators in Bismarck, North Dakota and another making freezers in Milwaukee, Wisconsin, part of the industrial conurbation on the shores of Lake Michigan. The problem to be discussed today is the pollution of the local river by the Bismarck factory, where low-level chemical waste draining from the factory into the water is having a damaging effect on plant and animal life for several miles downstream. This has been going on since the factory was first built, 33 years ago.

The first question is 'Does it matter?', since neither the unions nor the local authorities know about it or, if they do suspect, are too worried about the possible consequences to the local economy of the information being revealed (factory closure and job losses) to say anything. However, the journalist's request to visit the factory might indicate that the media are interested in finding out what's going on. If it is decided that the pollution must be stopped, something else must be done with the chemical waste. Can the waste just be boiled away, as is done in the Milwaukee factory? And should the toxic gases which this process would give off then be filtered away? Can the company afford the extra production costs this new process would create?

Business background

This situation might at first sight seem far-fetched, but it is based on real facts, albeit in a different country and in a different sort of business. Managers of firms do not automatically assume that pollution must be stopped at any price. And if it is stopped, it is more likely that it is because of the possible damage a scandal would do to the company's sales and reputation than because of the immorality of polluting the environment. Halting or reducing pollution does cost money and jobs, and any management would have to take this into account.

Outline of roles

A: The President: is worried about the risk of scandal, but also about the cost of stopping the pollution.

B: Marketing Manager: thinks radical action should be taken without delay to protect the up-market image of the firm.

C: Plant Manager, Bismarck: thinks nobody would be foolish enough to admit that pollution exists, and that if it has not been a problem for 33 years, why should it be now?

D: Chemical Engineer, Bismarck: will explain technical aspects – at Milwaukee (freezer factory), the waste is boiled away, adding 10% to production costs; this gas could be filtered, adding a further 5% to costs.

E: Financial Controller: suggests it might be better to close Bismarck plant and transfer production to Milwaukee.

F: Head of R and D: worried that if action is taken in Bismarck, it will have to be taken in Milwaukee too.

Possible outcome

This may depend on how shocked your learners are by the pollution. Younger students will be more inclined to stop the pollution or close the factory. The most likely outcome is to accept that action must be taken to stop or reduce pollution, given that the total cost (+15%) is not all that great. But a good Bismarck plant manager can sometimes succeed and persuade the others to do nothing.

Vocabulary

costly: expensive

downstream: the direction the water in the stream flows

to filter: to separate and remove a part of something

to find out: to discover

fuss: trouble, worry, concern

to leak out: to become known unexpectedly or unintentionally

the media: press, radio and television

out-of-the-way: far from the main centres

parent company: a company which owns and controls a subsidiary company by holding more than half its shares

to put paid to something: to put an end to something, to end all chances

sparsely populated: very few people

a subsidiary: a company owned and controlled by another company

toxic: poisonous

up-market: at the top end of the market, expensive and of high quality

waste: unwanted matter left after production

Sponsorship

Introduction

sponsorship

a household name

awareness

image-building

1. **Match the terms above with the correct definition below:**

a) the degree of public knowledge or recognition of a name, a product, or a company

b) a firm paying or giving financial help to an individual or organization to promote its products or services

c) taking action to improve customers' knowledge or appreciation of goods, services or a firm

d) a brand that is very widely known, bought or used

2. **Here are examples of use of the words above in context. Which word goes with which sentence?**

a) 'I was very lucky to get .... from Nike when I ran in the New York Marathon last year. I wore a Nike t-shirt and they gave money to a charity of my choice.'

b) 'Wherever you go in the world you can drink Coca-Cola: it's a ....'

c) 'You will never see one of our company's vans dirty or damaged; they are always clean and smart. This is part of our policy of ....'

d) Since Widget Motors started their television advertising campaign, the public's .... of their product has increased by 30%.

3. **Can you think of examples of companies or products that are household names? Are they household names everywhere, or just in your country?**

4. **Which activities depend heavily on sponsorship?**

5. **Do you know of sports or cultural activities for which players or artists earn more from sponsorship than from their fees?**

Business Roles
Sponsorship

© Cambridge
University Press
1997

Sponsorship

Situation

Your company produces water pumps for cars at a factory in Blackburn, England. You manufacture pumps for all the makes of car on sale in Europe. You are major suppliers of Rover and Nissan in England, and of Volkswagen in Spain, who fit your pumps to the engines of their new cars – this is known as the 'original equipment' market. You are also strong in the 'renewal' market in Europe, which is sales of pumps in garages and car shops for cars which need a replacement. Original equipment sales and renewal sales each account for about half of your turnover. The company and the product are both called 'Freeman's'.

Freeman's is a profitable firm making a good quality product. You are, however, over-dependent on Rover, Nissan and Volkswagen, and it would be wise for you to find more customers amongst other car manufacturers. Furthermore, your product is not a household name: few car owners demand a Freeman's when they need a new water pump, and few garages specifically recommend a Freeman's, although many stock them.

At the moment, your image-building and sales effort are based on the quality of your products, on the efforts of your sales force, on displays in shops and at trade exhibitions, and on advertising in car magazines.

The subject of today's meeting is this problem of public awareness of your company, its name, and most important of all, your products. You need to find a strategy for getting big orders from other car manufacturers, and for encouraging car shops, garages and car owners specifically to recommend or demand a Freeman's water pump when their pump needs changing.

You must decide:

- what the best ways of achieving these aims would be (television advertising, sponsorship, or no change in present policy?)

- if sponsorship in particular is effective, and good value for money

- and, if it is, exactly who you should sponsor and how much you should invest in sponsorship

---

Photocopiable

Business Roles
Sponsorship

© Cambridge
University Press
1997

Fact sheet

Major car manufacturers in Europe

Britain:	Germany:	France:	Italy:	Spain:	Sweden:
Ford	Audi	Citroën	Alfa Romeo	Ford	Saab
Honda	BMW	Peugeot	Fiat	Opel	Volvo
Jaguar	Ford	Renault	Lancia	Seat	
Nissan	Mercedes			Volkswagen	
Rover	Opel				
Toyota	Volkswagen				
Vauxhall					

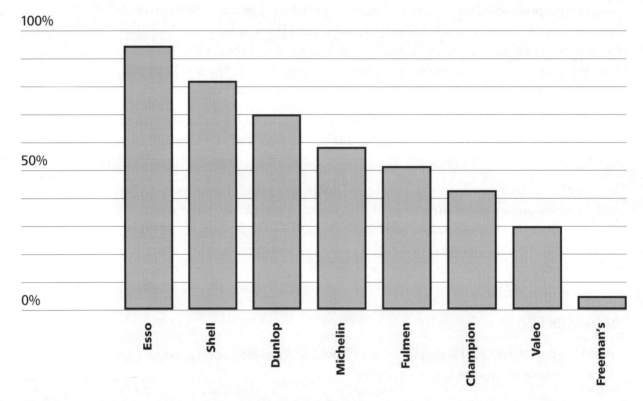

Awareness of Freeman's pumps compared to other firms'
products for the car.

Business Roles
Sponsorship

© Cambridge
University Press
1997

a

Role: **The Managing Director**

Chairing the meeting: Make sure everyone participates, and listen to all points of view. Write up important facts, questions and arguments on the board. Organize the meeting in the following way:

1. First analyse the problem. Why are Freeman's pumps not a household name? Why does this matter?

2. Then list possible solutions to the problem, paying particular attention to cost and effectiveness.

3. Finally, choose the best strategy to adopt.

Your own point of view: You have been very successful in increasing productivity and profits. You feel that communication in general, and image-building and sponsorship in particular, are 'fads', and don't like spending money on them.

However, you do recognize that in spite of definite improvements in the quality of your pumps, sales to major manufacturers have suffered from a lack of awareness. And you felt very offended recently when you met a director from Opel, for when you said you were the Managing Director of Freeman's, he said 'Oh, do you mean the furniture store?'.

b

Role: **The Communications Manager**

You want to build up the image and awareness of the company for the following reasons:

- your customers are satisfied with your products, but people do not 'think' Freeman's: they do not automatically associate your brand name with water pumps for cars

- you think your company excels in productivity, profitability, quality and 'just-in-time' production and supply to Rover, Volkswagen and Nissan. However, you do very little business with other major manufacturers such as Ford, Honda and Vauxhall.

- car manufacturers insist you put their names on your product, while refusing to specifically recommend Freeman's pumps as replacement parts.

Consequently, in addition to current marketing, you want to devote a big budget to sponsorship. You strongly favour sponsorship rather than other forms of advertising, because it is relatively inexpensive and would be very effective in making your name more widely known. Candidates for sponsorship are:

- a top football club (estimated cost £1 million per year)
- a television soap opera or quiz show (£500,000)
- the Blackburn Opera (£250,000)
- a major charity, such as the RSPDE (the Royal Society for the Prevention of Damage to the Environment) (£250,000)

You reckon you will need a budget of two million pounds per year for sponsorship. This represents about 1% of turnover and means doubling the money spent on marketing, sales and advertising. You are confident that with this budget you could increase sales by 50% in five years.

Role: **The Financial Controller**

C You are quite satisfied with profits, production, quality and everything else in the company, and refuse to waste money by spending it on passing fashions from the communications department. You are convinced that extra spending on communication will mean lower profits and investment, and be unpopular with shareholders; it might even damage the image of the company instead of improving it. Sponsorship can have a negative effect: what happens if the football club you sponsor loses a lot of matches – or even worse, its supporters get involved in football hooliganism? And what benefit can the company possibly draw from associations with charities, or opera?

You already spend two million pounds a year (1% of your turnover of £200 million) on your sales effort and on advertising. This is quite enough – you would be most unhappy about increasing this budget.

Role: **The Personnel Manager**

d You are very much in favour of sponsorship. You have difficulty finding qualified staff to work in the Blackburn factory, despite high unemployment in the area. You think this is because when your employees say 'I work at Freeman's', people say 'Where?'. Even in Blackburn itself, people don't know what the firm makes.

So you would particularly like to sponsor the local opera company, Blackburn Opera, but think you should also sponsor the football club, Blackburn Rovers.

You would also like the firm to get involved in sponsorship of events related to cars. Formula One motor racing is probably too expensive, but you would like Freeman's to sponsor Jaguar cars competing in the Le Mans 24-hour motor race in France. For a one million pound investment, this would give you widespread coverage on television.

Role: **The Production Manager**

f You are in charge of production at the factory in Blackburn. You understand arguments about awareness of the firm and its products, but think that these problems are of secondary importance in comparison to matters of production and sales. You have done, you feel, a very good job in the last few years increasing productivity and quality, and this has enabled the company to make more profits.

If the company really feels a need for raising awareness through sponsorship, you would like to sponsor a European event of some sort. How about a car race, like the Le Mans 24-hour race, or a powerboat race on the Mediterranean? The event should be linked to your products in some way, and get wide coverage on television. It would not be costly: sponsorship of a powerboat race would cost only about £500,000 – a big saving on the cost of television advertising.

Role: **The Marketing Manager**

You believe the firm has two major challenges for the next five years:

- You are over-dependent on Nissan and Rover and must try to get new contracts, with Toyota and Honda in particular because they have factories in England. You have got production and quality right, and it is now time to devote resources to winning new contracts with new manufacturers.

- You want to become leader on the renewal market, and feel this can only be done through better advertising (at the moment you are number two in Britain with 23% of the market, and in Europe your market share is 13%).

You are against a sponsorship deal with one particular car maker, as this might alienate the others. You think your magazine ads could and should be more effective – perhaps you need to find a new advertising agency? – and you are very much in favour of television advertising as a means of making Freeman's a household name. You think advertising in car magazines is much too limited. To make a 15-second television commercial and show it twenty times at peak viewing times could cost as little as two million pounds. This should lead to an increase in renewal sales of 20%.

Role: **The Sales Manager**

You sell to two quite distinct kinds of customers – car makers, and garages, car shops and car owners. The first are interested in 'just-in-time' delivery to the factories, in price, and in quality. The others are mostly interested in availability of stock when a pump needs changing.

You agree that there is an awareness problem. Several major car makers (BMW, Peugeot, Fiat) in Europe never buy your products, and few renewal buyers insist on having a 'Freeman's'.

Perhaps you could sponsor some event in association with a luxury product, such as champagne or perfume, in order to get across an idea of quality. And what about something cultural, like a film festival or an opera? This sort of sponsorship would be inexpensive. A film festival or an opera would be delighted with £250,000 and this would give you media coverage all over Europe.

Sponsorship

In brief

A manufacturer of water pumps for cars, based in Blackburn, England, must decide how to increase awareness of its products. The Communications Manager in particular is keen on developing sponsorship as a way of doing this – but just who or what should they sponsor?

Structure and procedure of the simulation

Introduction (optional) – 15-20 minutes

Preparation – 15-20 minutes

Simulation – 30-60 minutes

Follow-up (optional) – 15-20 minutes

Introduction

Answers

1. sponsorship (b)
    a household name (d)
    awareness (a)
    image-building (c)

2. a) sponsorship
    b) a household name
    c) image-building
    d) awareness

3. *possible answers* (these can be products or companies or both): Sony, Toyota, Nestlé, Canon, Schweppes, Seven-Up, Nikon, McDonald's, Philips, IBM, Kellogg's Cornflakes, Kodak, Benetton, Marks and Spencer, BP, Hoover. There will be variations according to where you are teaching and where your learners are from.

4. *possible answers*: motor racing, cycling, football, athletics, snooker, cultural events such as music concerts, theatre and art exhibitions, fund-raising events for charity.

5. *possible answers*: tennis, football, rugby, cricket, athletics.

Questions 1 and 2 concentrate on four key words which learners will need to understand and use in the discussion. The words are very interrelated. Sponsorship is a means of image-building and increasing awareness. The aim of increasing awareness is often (but not only) to make a product into a household name. If your product is already a household name, you will not need to increase awareness of the brand, but you still might wish to increase awareness of the company. You will certainly continue sponsorship (and advertising, of course) in order to maintain market share and fight off competitors.

Preparation

See 'General notes for teachers', p 2, for details on preparing learners for the simulation.

Note: The Communications Manager must be a keen and competent learner.

Give out the fact sheet, if you intend to use it. The names of European-based car manufacturers are given to help learners to know which companies a parts maker like Freeman's could hope to supply. The graph, comparing awareness of Freeman's as opposed to other firms on the motor vehicle parts sector, gives participants figures and therefore arguments to use in the discussion about awareness.

Simulation

See 'General notes for teachers', p 2, for details on managing the simulation.

Follow-up

See 'General notes for teachers', p 2, for details on feedback techniques and evaluation.

Summary of story

Freeman's is a maker of water pumps for cars, based in Blackburn in England. It supplies water pumps to car manufacturers (its best customers are Rover and Nissan in England, and Volkswagen in Spain) and to garages and car shops for replacement.

Today's meeting is to decide how to increase awareness of the company and its product, in order to increase market share and to make Freeman's a household name. Some participants think current strategies are adequate, some suggest increasing advertising, and some suggest sponsorship. But it is not enough to agree on the principle of sponsorship: the question will remain 'sponsorship of what?'.

If you have seven participants, this is what will be suggested for increasing awareness:

● television advertising
● sponsorship of:
   a football club
   a television soap opera or quiz show
   a major charity
   Jaguar cars competing in the
      Le Mans 24-hour race
   a powerboat race on the Mediterranean
   a film festival
   an opera
   a luxury product, e.g. champagne or perfume

Business background

It is the ambition of all major manufacturing or service companies to become a household name. If your products or services are not household names, you will be seeking the best means to make them into just that. For those manufacturers who supply products to retailers or manufacturers of finished goods, as Freeman's do in the simulation, the main obstacle is frequently that the companies they supply will want to put their own name on those products, rather than the name of the original producer; this means that an opportunity to impress the producer's name on the public, and to increase their profit margins, is lost.

To increase awareness, build their image, and make their products into a household name, firms constantly adjust prices, quality, specifications, and sales and marketing policy. More than anything, they advertise in the media, at exhibitions, and in shops. But increasingly, they sponsor sports, charities and cultural events. This is not because they are philanthropic, but because sponsorship can be cheaper and more effective than advertising. The company's name is seen and heard by a greater number of people, and its sponsoring of events for the public leads, consciously or unconsciously, to positive feelings about its products, both of which can mean increased sales.

Outline of roles

A: Managing Director: thinks communication is a fad, but admits company suffers from lack of awareness.

B: Communications Manager: wants to devote big budget to sponsorship to get people to think automatically of Freeman's when dealing with water pumps for cars, to get more major car makers as customers, and to get the name 'Freeman's' onto pumps fitted in new cars.

C: Financial Controller: thinks ideas from communications department are a waste of money and that sponsorship can backfire.

D: Personnel Manager: thinks greater awareness would help to find qualified staff.

E: Marketing Manager: wants new customers amongst car makers, and to become leader in the renewal market through television advertising.

F: Production Manager: feels communication problems are of secondary importance.

G: Sales Manager: would like to sponsor something cultural, or a luxury product.

Possible outcome

A good Communications Manager will probably persuade the others that sponsorship is a good idea. The outcome is less obvious when it comes to the question of 'sponsorship of what?'. There are good arguments against a football club (which might lose its matches rather than win them) or anything luxurious or cultural (the strange association of luxury or culture and water pumps). Sponsorship of a television show would be very expensive. A charity or something related to cars (Le Mans) or motors (powerboats) are likely to be chosen.

Vocabulary *(see also Introduction)*

ads: short form of advertisements

to alienate: to cause someone to turn against you

availability: how easily you can obtain the product

cost-effective: gives good results considering the cost

to devote resources to: to spend time or money on

a fad: a craze or passing fashion

hooliganism: threatening or violent behaviour against people or property; often used to describe violent behaviour by supporters during or after a football match

Jaguar: a British manufacturer of luxury cars

just in time: an organisation of production which consists of delivery of parts immediately before assembly in order to eliminate the need for stock

Le Mans: a city in the west of France where there is an annual 24-hour car race

Opel: one of the marques of cars made in Europe by General Motors, the American car manufacturer (the other is Vauxhall)

over-dependent: to rely too much on something

a soap opera: a long-running television series, usually shown several times a week, about the lives and problems of a specific group of characters

a venture: an undertaking, an event

wide coverage: a lot of exposure, frequent appearances

Who should we take over?

Introduction

With your partner, discuss what factors different people in a company would think important when looking for another firm to take over. Look at the list of personnel and write at least one factor next to each post:

CEO: ....

Marketing Manager: ....

Production Manager: ....

Financial Director: ....

Personnel Manager: ....

I.T. Manager: ....

Communications Manager: ....

Sales Manager: ....

Now compare your ideas with those of the rest of the group. Decide together on the <u>three</u> most important criteria for choosing a firm to take over.

Business Roles
Who should we take over?

© Cambridge University Press 1997

Who should we take over?

Situation

You work for 'La SBE' – La Sociéte Belge d'Electricité (The Belgian Electrical Company). Your company makes electric motors of two basic kinds – heavy motors for products like lifts, forklift trucks and electric vehicles, and light motors for equipment such as washing machines, electric drills, dishwashers, and vacuum cleaners. As the market for light motors is very competitive, it is important for the profitability of your company to maintain a balance in production between large and small motors.

It's quite a big firm: you have a workforce of over 4,000, and factories all over Europe – two in Italy, one in Spain, and three in Belgium. Your best market is Italy, but sales in Benelux and Spain are nearly as high and Germany and Britain are also big customers.

There are more than 40 firms in Europe making the same kind of motors, and imports from the Far East are taking an increasingly greater share of the market. Although you are the number two in Europe, you only have about 8% of the market. Most analysts think that in a few years many of the small manufacturers will either go out of business, or be taken over.

Within your company it is generally agreed that since productivity is very good in your factories, and since it is very difficult for you to increase market share without cutting your profits, the way ahead is for you to take over other competitors. You have recently taken over the factories in Italy and in Spain, and your aim is to become the European market leader.

You are meeting today to come to a decision on who to take over next. You have not got detailed information about the profits and turnover of the different firms you might want to buy, but you can make a preliminary decision on a firm or firms that you are interested in.

You must decide:

• which markets you most need to concentrate on

• where you need increased production facilities

• which competitor(s) you should aim to take over

Business Roles
Who should we take over?

© Cambridge
University Press
1997

Location of the SBE Group head office, factories, and candidates for takeover

Name	Country	Information	Pros and cons

Business Roles
Who should we take over?

© Cambridge University Press 1997

Role: **The CEO**

a

Chairing the meeting: You are the Chief Executive Officer of the company. You chair the meeting, and make sure everyone speaks. Organize the meeting in the following way:

1. List on the board the candidates for takeover, where they are situated, and anything the participants know about their financial situation.

2. Start the main part of the debate, which will consist of argument about the pros and cons of taking over the different candidates. Write up the strong and weak points of each candidate on the board.

Your own point of view: As an ambitious person, you personally would like to take over the German market leader, Sunnschein. This would make your company the undisputed number one in Europe.

Business Roles
Who should we take over?

© Cambridge University Press 1997

Role: **The Financial Manager**

b

You favour making a bid for Sunnschein, the leader in the German electric motor market. You know the President is very keen to take over this company, and you are very anxious to remain in his or her favour.

There are other arguments in favour of this move. These are:

• Germany is the only major market where you have no factories

• Sunnschein is the number six in Europe, so if you took them over, you would immediately become the number one

• Sunnschein has big contracts with major German firms such as Miele and Bosch

• Sunnschein has been having difficulties, and is losing money at the moment, so it would be a good time to buy

Business Roles
Who should we take over?

© Cambridge University Press 1997

Role: **The Marketing Manager**

c

You admit that sales in Germany are not as good as they should be, but think a takeover of Sunnschein would be a mistake. Here are your reasons:

- Sunnschein is in trouble. Last year they made record losses; they were forced to make 500 people redundant, and their productivity is very low

- German customers like to buy from German firms. You feel that if you take over Sunnschein, they will lose their contracts with Bosch and Miele

As a marketing person, you think the Spanish market is much more important. According to forecasters you have consulted recently, growth in the Spanish electric motors market will be the strongest in Europe in the next five years, and two of your important customers – Black and Decker, and Philips – are building new plant in Spain.

The best thing, therefore, would be to take over a Spanish firm. What about Torredos? They are very strong on the household electrical goods market (dishwashers, electric drills), and if you took them over, it would give you a dominant position in this area.

Business Roles
Who should we take over?

© Cambridge University Press 1997

Role: **The Director of Human Resources**

d

You have found it difficult to integrate the Italian and Spanish subsidiaries in the last few years. The Italian firms were taken over in 1988 and 1989 and the Spanish factory, which is a very modern one, in 1994.

The Italian firms were taken over when they were in big financial trouble, so they were relieved to be saved. However, the Spanish are not very cooperative in their day-to-day dealings with head office in Belgium, as they reckon their products are better than Belgian ones. More important from your point of view, they say that there is a nice family atmosphere in their factory which you will spoil with your emphasis on productivity and profits.

You are therefore not at all keen on taking over another Spanish firm. You're not too keen on Sunnschein either: it would be just too big for you to manage, as their firm is almost as big as yours, with nearly 3,000 employees.

So you are really against taking over anyone for the moment. You would prefer a breathing space of a couple of years. However, if this is not possible, you would suggest taking over a British firm. How about CGE, who are in financial difficulty, but have big contracts with Hoover?

Business Roles
Who should we take over?

© Cambridge University Press 1997

Role: **The Production Manager**

You naturally look at this question from the point of view of production. You see two major problems:

> The first is the imbalance of your European production structure – you need production facilities in Britain and Germany, which is where a lot of your customers are.

> The second is the fact that you need to keep a balance between your light and heavy motors. You are over-dependent on light motors for household goods, and this market is very competitive and not very profitable. You would like the firm you take over to be a builder of heavy motors for forklift trucks, electric vehicles and so on.

You therefore wish to avoid taking over a major competitor, as this would create an even greater imbalance in your production. You would go for two or three small competitors in Britain or Germany. How about Bolton Electric (they make forklift truck motors) or Madeburg Motor (electric vehicle motors)?

Role: **The Sales Manager**

These are the percentages of sales to different countries:

Italy 20%
Benelux 19%
Spain 17%
Germany 14%
Britain 13%
France 5%
Sweden 3%
others 5%
outside Europe 4%

You know that your colleagues will argue that you have no production facilities in Britain and Germany, but you don't think this is very important. What *is* important is making the best product at the cheapest price, and if you do this you will make inroads into the important German and Spanish markets, wherever the motors are produced. You have heard that Torredos in Spain have very low production costs, and that CGE in Britain have done a lot to improve their quality in recent years. Why not consider one (or both) of these for takeover?

Role: **The Quality Control Manager**

You have done a lot to improve the quality of your products in the last few years. The Belgian products have slowly improved, and the Italians are much better than they were, although it should be said that when you took their factory over their quality was poor. You've had trouble with the Spanish factory, who think their quality is quite good enough, and that in any case it's none of your business how good or bad their quality is.

You would therefore be very reluctant to take over another Spanish firm. You have a lot of admiration for the high quality of German products, and would be delighted to take over one of their firms.

Who should we take over?

In brief

A Belgian manufacturer of electric motors, which already has subsidiaries in Spain and Italy, has decided to take over another firm. Executives of the firm meet to discuss which company to buy, in which country. There are candidates in Germany, Spain and Britain.

Structure and procedure of the simulation

Introduction (optional) – 15-20 minutes

Preparation – 15-20 minutes

Simulation – 30-60 minutes

Follow-up (optional) – 15-20 minutes

Introduction

Answers

Suggested answers:

CEO: a big enough firm to make the new group market leader, a well-known firm for the prestige.

Marketing Manager: a firm with a good market share on markets where your own firm is weak or not present.

Production Manager: a firm with spare production capacity which you can use for manufacture of your leading products.

Financial Director: a profitable firm to help increase your profits, or quite the opposite, a firm in difficulty which will be cheap to buy.

Personnel Manager: a company with highly-trained (but low-paid?) staff you can 'poach' and transfer to other factories or offices.

I.T. Manager: a company which uses software compatible with yours.

Communications Manager: a company with a good image to bolster your image, or in search of awareness, which might make it easy to integrate into your strategy of corporate culture.

Sales Manager: a competitor you can then close down and so eliminate.

Use these or your own examples if your learners need help. For the group discussion, split large groups up into smaller ones of five or six.

Preparation

See the section 'General notes for teachers', p 2, for details on preparing learners for the simulation.

Simulation

See the section 'General notes for teachers', p 2, for details on managing the simulation.

Follow-up

See the section 'General notes for teachers', p 2, for details on feedback techniques and evaluation.

Summary of story

A Belgian, and very European, manufacturer of electric motors feels that it cannot expand or become more profitable by increasing sales of its own products or increasing prices, so it is looking for a competitor to take over. The question is not *if* it should take over another firm, but *who* it should take over. The candidates are British, German and Spanish. The firm already has Spanish and Italian subsidiaries.

Pros and cons of candidates if all seven roles are used:

Sunnschein, Germany:
+ would make SBE no. 1 in Europe; Germany is only major market where SBE has no factories; Sunnschein has major contracts with big German firms; would be cheap to buy at moment; makes good quality products; SBE needs production facilities in Germany

– Sunnschein is in trouble; big contracts might be lost if firm were no longer German; too big for SBE to handle

Madeburg Motor, Germany:
+ presence on important German market; small firm (easy to handle); would create balance between light and heavy motors

Torredos, Spain:
+ forecasters predict growth in Spain will be strongest in coming years; two of SBE's customers are building plant in Spain; Torredos is strong on household goods market

– Spanish firm taken over in 1994 was difficult to integrate into group; SBE already has Spanish factory

CGE, UK:
+ contracts with Hoover; cheap to buy; importance of UK market

– in financial difficulty

Bolton Electric, UK:
+ would create balance in SBE group between heavy and light motors; presence on important British market; small firm so cheap to buy and easy to handle

Business background

Firms take over other firms for a wide variety of reasons. It can be to increase market share; to create a big enough unit to be competitive; to get access to new technology; to eliminate a competitor; to break up the firm taken over and sell it off at a profit; to rationalize production; to make savings on supplies by placing larger orders; to acquire factories in areas with lower wages, and many more such reasons.

In this simulation the reason is given, and is quite clear: the firm has a strategy of external expansion, that is, it wants to get bigger and increase market share and profits by taking over a competitor.

There is nothing contradictory about a firm being number one in its own country and being in financial difficulty, like Sunnschein. This situation sometimes occurs, and makes the company in question an obvious target for takeover.

Outline of roles

A: CEO: wants to take over Sunnschein to make company the number one in Europe.

B: Financial Manager: also favours Sunnschein, in order to have a factory in Germany and get contracts with German firms, and because it would not be expensive to buy at the moment.

C: Marketing Manager: is against buying Sunnschein, due to its financial problems; favours Torredos, a Spanish firm, due to the increasing importance of the Spanish electric motor market.

D: Director of Human Resources: wants to avoid another Spanish firm, due to difficulties with Spanish factory taken over in 1994; thinks Sunnschein in Germany would be too big to handle. Would prefer a break from takeovers, but if required would recommend the British firm CGE, which is in financial difficulty.

E: Production Manager: wants better balance in production locations and between making light and heavy motors; suggests therefore either Bolton Electric in Britain (forklift truck motors) or Madeburg Motor in Germany (lawn motor mowers).

F: Sales Manager: believes producing high quality products at lowest production costs is paramount, and so favours Torredos in Spain, where production costs are low, and/or Bolton Electric in Britain, where quality is high.

G: Quality Control Manager: favours taking over a German firm; is against a Spanish firm.

Possible outcome

The participants in the meeting all have valid but contradictory arguments, so the outcome of the discussion is very open; much depends on how well individuals argue their cases. Sunnschein has perhaps slightly more chance than the other companies of being chosen; the CEO is in favour of it as well, which could tip the balance.

Vocabulary

breathing space: a period in which you recover from something

forecasters: people who predict what is going to happen

forklift truck: a small vehicle which lifts and transports goods around factories

imbalance: a lack of balance

to make a bid: to make an offer to buy or take over

to make inroads (into a market): to gain an increasingly larger share of a market

to make record losses: to lose more money than ever before

to make workers redundant: to dismiss workers in order to reduce the workforce

over-dependent: to rely too much on something

production facilities: machinery, factories, everything used for manufacturing

to take over: to buy, and so take control of, a firm

undisputed number one: unquestionably the leader, the biggest

Quality and personnel

Introduction

The aim of your company is total quality: the best possible quality for every product, service, action, communication, department and level. What do you do in these situations and why?

1. Your latest sales brochure contains a spelling mistake. Do you:

a) hope nobody notices?
b) have it reprinted?
c) correct the mistake by hand?
d) sack the person responsible?

2. One of your factories has consistently more faulty products than the others. Do you:

a) close it down?
b) invest heavily in more machinery?
c) appoint a new quality manager?
d) consult the trade unions about the problem?

3. Customers complain that your switchboard operator is always rude. Do you:

a) send him on a training course?
b) replace him with an automatic switchboard with music?
c) do nothing, because he acts as a filter for unimportant calls?
d) hire someone else to do the job?

4. The budget for washing your fleet of vans has gone up again. Do you:

a) decide it is worth it because of the good image it gives of the company?
b) stop washing your vans?
c) get the drivers to wash them themselves?
d) repaint the vans a colour which does not show the dirt?

5. Your workers are demanding company help for sports activities. Do you choose:

a) football, to develop team spirit in the firm?
b) judo, to develop a competitive spirit in the firm?
c) jogging, because it won't cost much?
d) cycling, because nearly everyone will be able to join in?

6. To improve worker involvement do you:

a) install 'ideas boxes' in which employees can insert their ideas written on pieces of paper?
b) set up 'quality circles'?
c) change working methods so employees participate in the complete production process?
d) inform workers of all important decisions in a monthly newsletter?

Business Roles
Quality and personnel

© Cambridge University Press 1997

Quality and personnel

Situation

Your company makes video cassette recorders (VCRs). The name of the company and the products is Nagoya, the same as the city where the head office and Japanese factory are based. You also have a factory in Newport, Wales.

You are in a highly competitive market. You compete with the Japanese giants, with competitively-priced South Korean products and with European VCRs. Your market share in Europe is small, but growing slowly.

There is one problem: quality at the Newport factory. It's a very modern factory, opened only five years ago. It's actually more modern than the Japanese factory, and productivity is just as good as in Japan. However, quality is not as good; although the factory in Newport makes your up-market multi-standard VCRs, there are far fewer problems with the lower-priced, simpler products imported from Japan.

Latest figures for the total number of recorders sent back by users, or rejected after random checks at the end of the production line are:

Newport 1.02%
Nagoya 0.36%

Today you are meeting at the factory in Newport to find out why there are nearly three times as many defective products in Wales as in Japan.

You must decide:

• why there is such difference in quality between the two factories' products: just what is the problem?

• what can be done to bring the Newport factory up to Japanese standards

---

Fact sheet

Total number of defective products in last 12 months

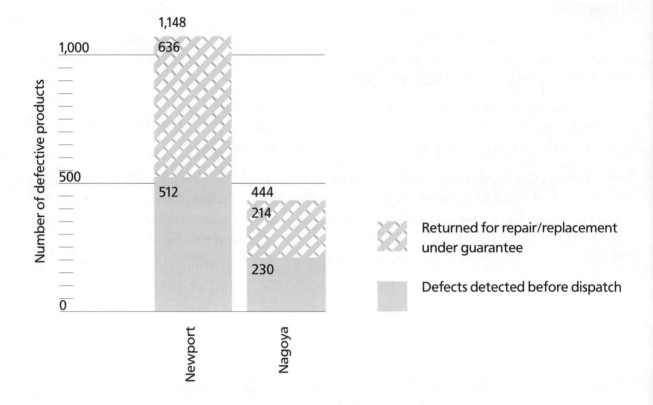

Reasons work hours lost last year in Newport

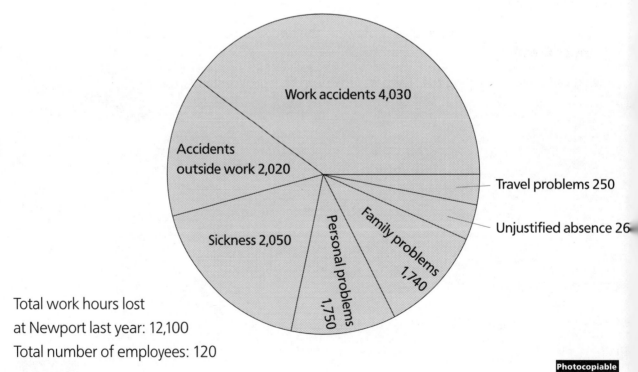

Total work hours lost
at Newport last year: 12,100
Total number of employees: 120

Business Roles
**Quality and
personnel**

© Cambridge
University Press
1997

a

Role: **The Managing Director**

Chairing the meeting: You chair the meeting and ensure everyone joins in. Organize the meeting in the following way:

1. First get the facts: what is this problem of poor quality in Newport due to? Why are things so much better in Japan?

2. Write on the board different solutions suggested, and then choose the best.

Your own point of view: You <u>must</u> solve this problem. You will lose markets if quality is not good enough. Investment in the Welsh factory, particularly in automation, has been heavy. You feel that the problem probably lies in industrial relations and working conditions.

Business Roles
Quality and personnel

© Cambridge University Press 1997

---

b

Role: **The Plant Manager, Newport**

The basic problem is one of human relations and worker involvement, participation and motivation. Your colleagues are too obsessed with productivity and returns on investment. Newport has always had a quality problem, but the firm has always concentrated on technical aspects, never on human aspects.

You have some concrete suggestions to make:

- improve safety: set an aim of zero accidents in three years' time

- improve health: improve the air conditioning and lighting, both of which the workers complain about

- improve working methods: have workers assembling the whole recorder from the start to the end of the process. Reduce the number of supervisory staff in the factory. Instead, make workers themselves responsible for the repair of machines

- improve quality bonuses

- set up a works council to meet in working hours

- give a few perks: subsidize sports activities and recreational activities

Business Roles
Quality and personnel

© Cambridge University Press 1997

Role: **The Production Manager, Newport**

C Your solution is a simple one, even if it might be costly in the short term. You are sure that there is a fundamental difference between the mentality of Japanese and Welsh workers. What works in Japan will probably not work here. You feel it is a waste of time trying to motivate the Newport workers, or to get them more involved in the production process. Bonus schemes and perks have already been tried, and did not work. It is no good hoping the British (it would be the same in any European country) will accept longer hours or fewer holidays.

So what you suggest is full automation of production. It is technically possible now, and the company should make it their aim to have no human workers in the factory at all in three years' time, only robots. This would certainly solve the quality problem.

Role: **The Corporate Head of Quality Control**

d You are reluctant to say this, but in the last analysis, the differences between the Welsh and Japanese factories are due to the attitudes of the workers. In Japan, the workers feel involved in the production process, are concerned about quality, are more motivated, and quite simply work harder, and for longer hours. They work, on average, five and a half days a week, and take only three weeks' holiday. There is probably scope for improving working conditions in Newport, and maybe better quality bonuses would help, but the real solution is to get the Newport workers to work harder and longer, and to raise their level of motivation and interest in their jobs to the same level as in Japan.

Role: **The Corporate Marketing Manager**

You do not know too much about the technical aspects of the quality problem. What you do know is that this problem must be solved quickly. How can you possibly market up-market Newport products under the same brand name as less expensive Nagoya-made products, when the former have more defects than the latter? This is very damaging for the image and reputation of the whole firm. Haven't the Newport workers already proved they are unable to match Japanese quality? Wouldn't it be better to try further automation and so reduce the number of defects at the same time as reducing the number of workers?

Role: **The Personnel Manager, Newport**

You have already tried to improve quality by improving worker participation, involvement and motivation. You tried an 'ideas box,' but the only suggestion you got was 'Cut the plant manager's salary'. You tried quality circles, but nobody wanted to stay after work to attend them. You tried quality bonuses, but the workers said they were too small. And you put a new net on the tennis court behind the factory, and still almost nobody plays.

All the workers want is higher pay and longer holidays, and you know these demands are quite unrealistic.

Role: **The Plant Manager, Nagoya**

You know why quality is better in Japan. Workers there feel much more involved in the company, and are therefore much more motivated when it comes to improving quality. Your workers are happy in their jobs, and most of them will spend their whole working life with you. Newport should make it their aim to incite their workers to feel the same. Bonuses and perks, as well as working conditions in general, are better in Japan. Newport should be brought up to the same standards, and then quality will improve.

Management methods are also better in Nagoya. The wage differences are smaller between management and workers, and managers mix and work with their staff much more readily in Japan. Here again, Newport could simply copy Nagoya.

Quality and personnel

In brief

A Japanese firm makes video recorders in Nagoya, Japan, and in Newport, Wales. You are meeting today to try to solve the quality problem you have in the Newport factory, where the number of defective products is much greater than at the Nagoya plant.

Structure and procedure of the simulation

Introduction (optional) – 15-20 minutes

Preparation – 15-20 minutes

Simulation – 30-60 minutes

Follow-up (optional) – 15-20 minutes

Introduction
This is in the form of a questionnaire. It is designed to get learners talking about the subject to be discussed in the simulation at the same time as using some of the vocabulary from the situation and roles.

In a large group, do this as pairwork first, and then, when the pairs have chosen all their answers, discuss as a group. There are no 'right' answers to the questions. Discussion will ensue as soon as you ask learners to justify their choices.

Preparation
See the section 'General notes for teachers', p 2, for details on preparing learners for the simulation.

Note: Give out the fact sheet with the simulation. Give role B to a competent student, as this is a key role.

Simulation
See the section 'General notes for teachers', p 2, for details on managing the simulation.

Follow-up
See the section 'General notes for teachers', p 2, for details on feedback techniques and evaluation.

Summary of story

Nagoya, a Japanese maker of video cassette recorders, has factories in Japan and in Wales. The aim of the meeting today is to find out why it is that the quality of the Welsh products is inferior to that of the Japanese products, and to decide what to do about it. What is puzzling about this quality problem is that Newport is a more modern factory than Nagoya and the firm has spent more there on automation than in Japan.

At one extreme the position is that the only solution lies in full automation and having no workers at all in a few years. At the other extreme it is thought that the whole quality problem can only be solved by a more human approach which would motivate the workers better.

Business background

In recent years, many businesses have tried to develop a policy of 'total quality' and 'zero defects'. The latter is usually just an aim, because it is impossible to achieve. The former involves everyone in the firm in offering the best possible quality at every stage of production as well as in every area of business, including such things as how employees answer the telephone or how quick the after-sales service is.

But different firms have gone about pursuing these objectives in different ways. Basically, there are two possible approaches. The first consists in maximizing productivity, often with the help of heavy investment in machinery and electronics. The second combines this approach with an 'enlightened' policy on personnel management, seeking to involve employees at all levels of the hierarchy in all aspects of production and of decision-making.

Outline of roles

A: Managing Director: wonders if further automation *is* the answer, as it hasn't worked up to now.

B: Plant Manager, Newport: thinks the problem is definitely one of human relations and worker involvement; has precise proposals for improving safety, health, working methods, bonuses and perks.

C: Production Manager, Newport: suggests full automation of factory within three years.

D: Corporate Head of Quality Control: wants Newport workers to work harder and for longer hours.

E: Corporate Marketing Manager: worried about poor quality damaging image of firm; thinks further automation would help.

F: Personnel Manager, Newport: claims s/he has already tried to improve industrial relations and working conditions, without success.

G: Plant Manager, Nagoya: wants Newport to copy Nagoya's working and industrial relation methods.

Possible outcome

There are good arguments for further automation, as some effort has been made already in improving working methods and industrial relations. However, the better quality in Japan would seem to prove that their working methods are better and should be adopted in Newport. If role B argues their case well, the decision should go their way, but it's not a forgone conclusion.

Vocabulary

bonus: extra pay for employees, in addition to their usual wages

competitively-priced: cheap enough to sell well

concrete suggestions: clear and specific suggestions

to cut a salary: to reduce it

full automation: all production done by machines

involvement: participation, association, partnership

mentality: way of thinking

multi-standard video recorder: a VCR that works with all three international video standards, PAL, SECAM and NTSC

obsessed with: thinking only of

perks: extra things a company gives workers in addition to their pay

quality circles: groups of workers and management who meet to discuss ways of improving production and quality

random checks: checks made every so often on a limited number of finished products

recreational activities: spare-time activities

scope: the opportunity for doing something

to subsidize: to support with financial help

up-market: at the top end of the market, expensive and of high quality

works council: a group of workers and management who meet regularly to discuss work and pay conditions

The chocolate factory

Introduction

Your company is going to build a new factory. Which of the following factors should be considered when choosing the site? With a partner, choose the <u>ten</u> most important factors for the company from this list:

availability of personnel

availability of subsidies

awareness of location (have people heard of this place?)

beauty of site

climate

cost of housing

cost of land

image of town, area, or country

labour costs

levels of pollution

location of competitors

location of your biggest markets and communications between them and the factory

proximity to a beach

proximity of suppliers

quality of facilities (schools, libraries, sports, crèches, etc.)

quality of public transport

rate of business taxes

social problems in area (drugs, crime, homelessness, etc.)

unemployment in the area

Now compare your list with other students in the class, and try to agree on <u>one</u> list of the ten most important factors. Number the list from 1 (the most important) to 10 (the least important).

Business Roles
The Chocolate Factory

© Cambridge University Press 1997

The chocolate factory

Situation

You work for Squarebush, the biggest chocolate and confectionery manufacturer in Australia, based in Geelong, Victoria. You have your head office and main factory in Geelong; you have another, smaller factory in Perth, Western Australia. You make all types of sweets and chocolates, and are market leader in confectioners and supermarkets.

Your company has decided to start making fresh, Belgian-style, handmade chocolates. You are going to open your own chain of shops in town centres all over Australia to sell them. Your new product will be a luxurious one, which is why you are going to retail them in your own exclusive outlets. One very special feature of the product is its freshness: some of the chocolates will contain fresh cream and customers will be advised to eat them within a week of buying them. They should never be kept more than three weeks from the date of manufacture.

You need to build a new factory to manufacture these chocolates, and are meeting today to choose a new site for the factory. These are the factors you must take into consideration in making your choice:

communications with the rest of Australia

availability of qualified personnel

cost of land

cost of housing for re-located personnel

conviviality of location for personnel

image of town and its effect on product image

labour costs

climate

the location of your biggest markets

You must decide:

- which of the locations suggested is the most suitable for the location of your new factory?

- what are the advantages of the site you propose?

- what are the disadvantages of the other sites?

Business Roles
The Chocolate Factory

© Cambridge University Press 1997

Fact sheet

Cost of factory space

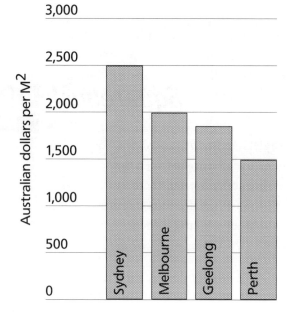

Labour costs

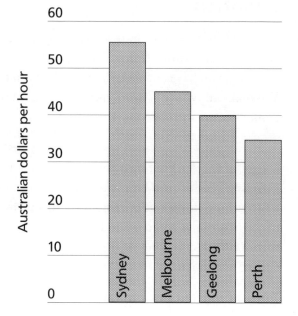

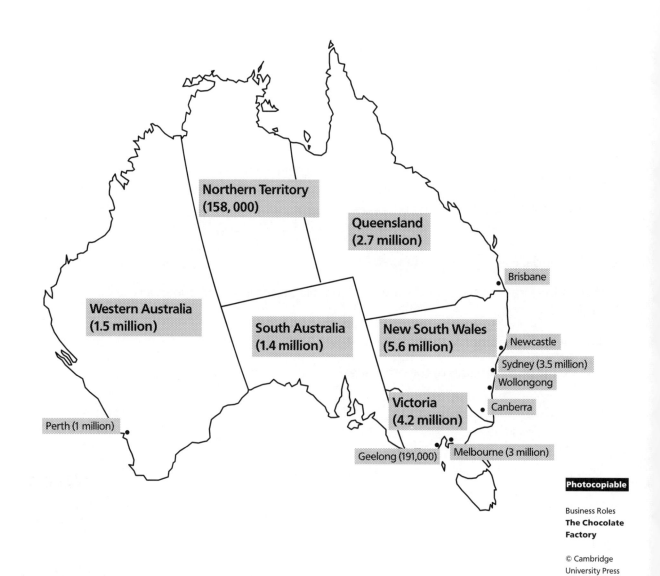

Business Roles
The Chocolate Factory

© Cambridge
University Press
1997

Role: **The Chief Executive**

a

Chairing the meeting: Organize the meeting in the following way:

1. On the board, list all the locations proposed.

2. Then list their advantages and disadvantages, and try to come to a conclusion.

The participants will disagree, at least initially, so as chairperson you will have to encourage them to compromise and try to guide the meeting towards a consensus.

Your point of view: You personally favour Melbourne as the location for the new factory. Communications with the rest of the country are good, unemployment is high, so there will be no shortage of qualified personnel, and labour costs will be reasonable. Melbourne is a big city, with excellent facilities. Finally, it's near Geelong, and so will be easy for you to reach from the head office.

Role: **The Marketing Manager**

b

You are the marketing manager, and are responsible for sales and distribution.

Because of this, you favour Sydney, which a quick look at the map will show to be right in the heart of the most populated areas of Australia, where you will open the most outlets for your chocolates and have an enormous market. Road, rail and air communications with the other big centres of population are excellent. Sydney is a big city with a pleasant climate, and has all the schools, shops and entertainment people need. There is no shortage of qualified labour, and not only is it the most populated city in the country but it is in the most populated state.

Role: **The Plant Manager, new factory**

c

You have worked for the company for ten years, and have been appointed as the plant manager of the new factory. You live in Geelong and don't want to move, so you argue in favour of building the new factory in the town. You think there are very good arguments for this choice:

Firstly, Geelong is a very nice town. It is big enough to have all the facilities you expect of a modern town, but small enough to be pleasant to live in. It is near the coast, and has a wonderful climate. Secondly, property is expensive, but as personnel would not need to be relocated this is not a problem. Land to build the factory on might be expensive, but the local authorities would certainly help you find a plot if you announced you were intending to create several hundred new jobs here. Lastly, as you already have a factory here, you already have some staff with the right experience and qualifications for your type of production.

Role: **The Production Manager**

You are the head office manager in charge of production in Geelong and Perth, and you will also be in charge of production in the new factory when it is built.

You favour Perth as the site for this new factory. You already have a factory there, and this would mean you could visit both factories during the same trip when you go to Perth, thus saving a lot of time and trouble.

You know the same argument applies to building the new factory in Geelong, but Perth is a big city with a lot of advantages for your company – a big local market, good communications with the rest of Australia, availability of qualified personnel – as well as the usual facilities such as schools, housing, entertainment and public transport. In addition, labour costs are lower than in the east of Australia, land for the factory site is cheaper, and housing for the workers is much less costly.

Business Roles
The Chocolate Factory

© Cambridge University Press 1997

Role: **The Personnel Manager**

You are the personnel manager from head office. You will have to find staff for the new factory and this will be difficult, whichever town is chosen. Unqualified operators will be easy to find wherever you go, but the engineers and technicians you will need will be more difficult to find. Some can be transferred from existing factories but they will then have to be replaced there.

You have no special preference for the moment, and will listen to arguments for and against all the proposed sites, and then try to come to a conclusion. You already have the following doubts about the places mentioned:

Sydney: very big, busy and expensive, all costs are likely to be highest – land, housing, labour

Geelong: too far from the big markets, not enough qualified personnel, especially as you already have a factory there

Perth: much too far from your main markets, unpleasant climate (too hot) – not ideal for making fresh chocolates

Melbourne: also big and expensive, and perhaps difficult to attract qualified personnel to, because they prefer the more cosmopolitan Sydney

Business Roles
The Chocolate Factory

© Cambridge University Press 1997

Role: **The Financial Director**

You are, naturally, worried about costs more than anything else. For this reason, you would favour Melbourne or Perth. Perth would be the cheapest for land to build the factory, for wage costs, and for housing for the personnel transferred there. Melbourne is cheaper than Sydney, and would have plenty of qualified engineers and technicians available, thus avoiding the costs involved in relocation.

Sydney is really too expensive from every point of view. Geelong is rather too small: its population is not big enough for it to meet your new needs in qualified staff, especially as you already have a factory there.

Business Roles
The Chocolate Factory

© Cambridge University Press 1997

Role: **The Head of Sales**

Looking at the map will indicate where <u>not</u> to locate the new factory. Your main customers are in the big cities and in the populous states of the east of Australia. It must be stressed that out of a total population of seventeen million people, over five and a half million live in the state of New South Wales and another four million in Victoria.

You have got to move fresh chocolates, with a shelf-life of only a week, in refrigerated transport to the great centres of population – the Sydney area (Sydney, Newcastle, Wollongong), the Brisbane area, the Melbourne area, and the Adelaide area. Perth would therefore seem out of the question. From your point of view there are strong arguments in favour of a new factory in the Sydney area.

Business Roles
The Chocolate Factory

© Cambridge University Press 1997

The chocolate factory

In brief

An Australian chocolate manufacturer must choose a site for its new factory, which will manufacture a new range of handmade products for its own specialist outlets. The head office and one factory are in Geelong, Victoria, and there is another factory in Perth, Western Australia. Both these towns are candidates for the new factory, together with Melbourne and Sydney.

Structure and procedure of the simulation

Introduction (optional) – 15-20 minutes

Preparation – 15-20 minutes

Simulation – 30-45 minutes

Follow-up (optional) – 15-20 minutes

Introduction

Give out the first task, which asks the learners to decide in pairs and then as a whole group on the most important factors in building a new factory. The pairwork could alternatively be done in small groups if you have a large class, or prepared beforehand as homework. Once the students have made their list in pairs, try to get the whole group to work out together a joint list of the ten most important factors, in order of importance.

The aim of the task is really to eliminate the factors of little or no importance and to focus on what the key factors are. Suggested factors of no importance are: beauty of site, proximity of a beach, climate, awareness of location, location of competitors. Suggested factors of less importance are: levels of pollution, quality of public transport, social problems in area, quality of facilities. The students will have their own views about key factors, which should lead to lively discussion as they try to agree on a class list. If you cannot reach agreement, don't worry: the important thing is to introduce your learners to the notions which will come up in the discussion later.

Preparation

See the section 'General notes for teachers', p 2, for details on preparing learners for the simulation.

Simulation

See the section 'General notes for teachers', p 2, for details on managing the simulation.

Follow-up

See the section 'General notes for teachers', p 2, for details on feedback techniques and evaluation.

Summary of story

An Australian chocolate manufacturer, Squarebush, is launching a new product – Belgian-style, handmade chocolates. These chocolates will be sold in specialist shops owned by the firm, which are being opened in all the main Australian cities. The chocolates will have a very short shelf-life and must be delivered and sold in a few days.

The new product will be produced in a new, purpose-built factory; the decision that needs to be taken is where this new factory will be located. There are four candidates – Geelong (where Squarebush already has their head office and main factory); Perth (where they also have a factory); Sydney; and Melbourne.

Here are the main arguments for and against each location:

Melbourne:
    for – availability of qualified personnel, facilities, near Geelong

    against – big, expensive, difficult to attract qualified staff

Sydney:
    for – location in heart of most populated area of Australia, good communications with rest of country, pleasant climate

    against – big, busy and expensive location

Geelong:
    for – convivial location, nice climate, one factory already located in town

    against – property expensive, land expensive, far from main markets, not enough qualified staff, too small

Perth:
    for – one factory already located in city, big city with good facilities, big local market, good communications, availability of qualified personnel, low labour costs, cheap land and housing

    against – too far from main markets, too hot

Business background

Deciding where to site a new factory is a decision many companies have to take. The reason given for the final choice of the site varies greatly from one company to another, and from one time to another. This is doubtless because a factor which could encourage one firm to choose a particular location might deter another firm from choosing the same place.

For example, already having a factory in one town might be seen as a reason for building the new factory in the same town because you know the place well and have qualified staff available locally. It could equally be seen as a reason for building elsewhere, because of the shortage of qualified staff if you have two factories in the same town.

If the geographical area you are interested in offers financial incentives such as subsidies, you might well be attracted because of them; on the other hand, you might feel that a place that needs to offer subsidies to attract businesses must have something wrong with it.

Outline of roles

A: Chief Executive: favours Melbourne, as it's close to Geelong and to the main markets.

B: Marketing Manager: favours Sydney, as it's right in the heart of the main markets.

C: Plant Manager, new factory: favours Geelong, because he or she does not really want to move.

D: Production Manager: favours Perth, because it's a big city with much lower costs than in the east.

E: Personnel Manager: undecided, but worried about the difficulties involved in finding qualified operators, wherever the factory will be.

F: Financial Director: favours Melbourne or Perth for reasons of cost.

C: Head of Sales: is against Perth; favours Sydney, as it has the biggest concentration of population and is therefore the biggest market.

Possible outcome

It is hard to predict the outcome. Perth is probably unlikely to be chosen, because it is so far from the main markets, and the transport of fresh chocolates in refrigerated containers would be costly. As for the other cities, it will depend on how good a case each participant argues for their location. Either Sydney or Melbourne are the most likely to be chosen, but Geelong is certainly a possibility.

Vocabulary

availability of personnel: whether there are enough workers on the job market

confectionery: sweets, candy

consensus: agreement of all present

market leader: firm which sells more of its products than any other manufacturer of the same products

outlet: shop

plot: piece of ground

qualified labour/personnel: trained workforce

relocation: moving employees to a new place of work

shelf-life: how long a perishable product can be kept on sale

shortage: lack

Integration

Introduction

1. Have you ever worked for, or do you know about, a firm which was taken over by another firm, or which took over another firm?

2. What problems arose because of this takeover:
    • for the firm taken over?
    • for the firm which did the taking over?

    How were these problems solved?

3. What do you think was learned from this experience?

4. What rules should be followed by the management of a company when they have just taken over another firm? Select the first most important:

Leave the managers of the subsidiary in their jobs

Appoint your own managers at the head of the subsidiary straight away

Invest massively in the new subsidiary

Sell off parts of the new subsidiary

Stop using the old brand names of the new subsidiary

Keep the old brand names of the new subsidiary

Rename the subsidiary with the new parent company name

Let the subsidiary keep its old name

Learn the language of the subsidiary's country

Offer the new employees language courses to learn your language

Abolish the new subsidiary's R and D department

Let the subsidiary do its own research

Harmonise product ranges

Keep separate product ranges

Harmonise pay rates

Keep different pay rates

Business Roles
Integration

© Cambridge
University Press
1997

Integration

Situation

You work for a major French cutlery manufacturer called Marquet, based in Thiers in the south of France. You are strong in the French domestic market, where you have an 8% share of the market for all types of cutlery, and 10% of the stainless steel market. You had found it hard to break into the European market, but have succeeded in recent years by taking over two firms, one Belgian and the other British. These firms are now subsidiaries of Marquet, but have kept a lot of autonomy in the running of their businesses.

The Belgian firm is called Tudor Rose, and has a factory near Bruges making cheap tin and aluminium products for campers, canteens and hospitals. The British firm is called Hawthorn, and has a factory in Sheffield. They manufacture high quality up-market silver cutlery with the brand name Hawthorn. Your head office and French factory are in Thiers, where you make mostly middle-range stainless steel cutlery.

When you took over the Belgian firm, you saved the factory from closure, and it proved very easy to integrate the Belgians into the Marquet structure. However, the situation is very different with the British firm. They welcome the investment you have made in new machinery to improve production, but are determined to remain as independent as possible. Head office managers in Thiers constantly complain about a complete lack of cooperation on the part of the managers at the Sheffield plant. You are meeting today to discuss this.

You must decide:

• is it true that the British are uncooperative, and if so, how and why?

• does it matter? What problems does it cause for the group?

• what can and should be done about it?

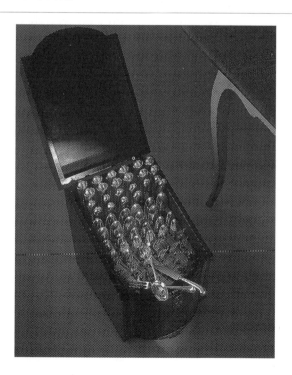

Business Roles
Integration

© Cambridge
University Press
1997

Role: **The President**

a

Chairing the meeting: Ask each participant to say if and how the British are uncooperative, and what problems this causes for the group. You need to be sure that this is not just a case of personal rivalry between managers. Once you have listed the real problems, concentrate on finding practical solutions to them.

Your own point of view: You have had several complaints from your senior managers about the uncooperative attitude of the Sheffield managers. You are determined to create an integrated European group, and are ready to appoint managers from France or Belgium to run the Sheffield plant if this is what is needed to solve the problem.

Business Roles
Integration

© Cambridge
University Press
1997

Role: **The Marketing Manager, head office**

b

Your strategy for the Marquet group is to increase sales of products from each country in the other two countries. So at the same time as increasing sales of French products in Britain, for instance, you are trying to increase sales of British products in France. The Belgians have used your marketing services to take a fair share of the French market. The British seem to want to 'do their own thing', and you get little cooperation from their marketing department.

Communication with the Sheffield people is not easy. Each time you visit their factory, they arrange for a taxi to take you back to the airport at 3 p.m., on the grounds that there might be heavy traffic on the motorway and extra security checks at the airport. As the earliest flight only gets you there at 11 a.m., you never have time to do all you need.

In addition, your English is not very good, yet your British counterparts seem to be making no effort to improve their French; this also makes communication difficult.

Business Roles
Integration

© Cambridge
University Press
1997

Role: **The Managing Director, British subsidiary**

C

You are not very happy in your job. Until the French took your firm over, you did what you wanted, and now they are always interfering and telling you to improve productivity. Surely the most important thing is profits, and your factory is the most profitable in the Marquet group; your up-market silver cutlery sells very well.

There is a nice family atmosphere in your factory, and you're worried the French will spoil everything. You've already been forced to lay off 50 workers – fortunately most could take early retirement. The canteen has been contracted out 'to save money' – so now the workers are complaining it costs more to eat worse food.

Head Office is always asking you for figures on sales, production, costs, and the workforce, and you really can't see what they need them for. They've even asked you to learn French, which seems daft, as they all speak reasonable English. So you have lessons, but you haven't made much progress – you find it difficult, and like the other managers you don't have time to attend the classes regularly.

Role: **The Director of Human Relations, head office**

d

The British are rather uncooperative, but you don't think it's all their fault. You know there is a language barrier: the French are having English lessons, and several of them have improved their English to quite a reasonable standard; the British are having French lessons, but they don't seem to attend them regularly, and their accents are very bad. If only you could get this right, communications would improve a lot.

It is true there is a nice family atmosphere in the Sheffield plant. It would be wise for the group to try to learn from the British in this respect, and concentrate on improving working methods through a strategy of good industrial relations. With this in mind, you are aiming at creating a 'Marquet group spirit', and have arranged for football and rugby matches to be played between teams from the different factories.

Role: **Marketing Manager, Sheffield**

You are not very happy with the new set-up. The people from Marquet are determined to create an integrated European marketing structure, with each country marketing the products of the other two. You think this is a terrible mistake from a marketing point of view, as your up-market products should not be mixed up, in the consumer's mind, with 'cheap' products from France and Belgium.

You admit that communications with head office are poor. You do not like the people from Thiers going round your factory and offices telling you how to do a job you know you can do better than them. And since their English is so good, why do they keep talking in French?

Role: **The Industrial Manager**

f You are the head office manager in charge of the three factories in Thiers, Sheffield and Bruges. You organize and coordinate production in each factory, and you are, in theory at least, the plant production manager's boss.

You have a real problem with Sheffield. The production manager there is extremely uncooperative, and regards him/herself as answerable only to the managing director of the British subsidiary. You need weekly production figures, and every week your secretary has to ring up and ask for them, otherwise you don't get them.

Productivity is not as good in Sheffield as it is in Thiers, but it is proving very difficult to get the British to change their working practices. You agree that their problems are not the same as the French or Belgian ones, but this is no reason to be uncooperative. They could learn a lot from you about production methods and could rapidly improve their productivity.

Role: **The Production Manager, Sheffield plant**

g You are the production manager for the British factory. You feel that complaints about you being uncooperative are absurd. It's true that you resent having to provide production figures every week for Thiers, but this is because you are sure that they will just be filed and ignored at head office.

You welcome Marquet's investment in new machinery and new production methods, but feel that you are quite capable, with this machinery, of increasing productivity at a satisfactory rate. You don't like the industrial manager from Thiers prowling round the factory, criticizing everything. You have visited the Thiers factory, which is old and dirty, and which has a poor industrial relations record, and you think that the French should improve things there before interfering in your business.

Role: **The Plant Manager, Bruges plant**

h You were pleased to be taken over by Marquet, as your firm would probably have been closed down otherwise. In addition, your parent company has invested heavily in new machinery for your factory, enabling you to improve productivity. Joining the Marquet group has also opened up the French and British markets for your products, at the same time as giving you a wider range of products to market in the Benelux countries: you now sell cutlery from all three of the group's factories. Basically, you are delighted to belong to a truly European group, and cannot understand why your British colleagues do not share your feelings.

Integration

In brief

A French cutlery manufacturer is finding the British firm it recently took over rather uncooperative. Personnel meet to try to find out in what ways the Sheffield factory is uncooperative, and to discuss what should be done about it.

Structure and procedure of the simulation

Introduction (optional) – 15-20 minutes

Preparation – 15-20 minutes

Simulation – 30-60 minutes

Follow-up (optional) – 15-20 minutes

Introduction

The questions in the task are designed to get the students thinking about the issues generated by the takeover of one firm by another. If no-one in the group has experience or much knowledge of takeovers, it might be helpful to concentrate on question 5. The ideas in this question are designed to provoke discussion at the same time as giving hints as to possible problems which may arise after a takeover. There are no 'right' answers to this question, as takeovers vary, but asking learners to explain their choice of rules should generate discussion. Do this task with the whole group unless you have a large class, in which case divide them up into groups of six or seven for discussion.

The 'Business background' gives ideas of possible problems that can arise when firms are taken over.

Preparation

See the section 'General notes for teachers', p 2, for details on preparing learners for the simulation.

Simulation

See the section 'General notes for teachers', p 2, for details on managing the simulation.

Follow-up

See the section 'General notes for teachers', p 2, for details on feedback techniques and evaluation.

Summary of story

A European manufacturer of cutlery has its head office in Thiers, France, and two subsidiaries: one British, based in Sheffield, the other Belgian, based in Bruges. Each site has a factory. The problem to be resolved today is the lack of cooperation on the part of the British.

French complaints: British are uncooperative, regard everything French do as interference, are reluctant to supply figures, have low productivity but do not want to change working practices, make no effort to learn French, and do everything they can to keep French visits to a minimum.

British complaints: French always interfering although British factory is the most profitable in the group, will spoil family atmosphere in Sheffield factory, always asking for figures, insist on British learning French although they speak good English, French factory is old and dirty and British have nothing to learn from them, and marketing policy is damaging Sheffield's up-market image.

Business background

When one company takes over another, there are always problems merging the companies harmoniously. The company which is bought up will usually feel resentful. Even if the two firms are in the same country, there will be a clash of cultures and working methods. This will be even more accentuated if the takeover involves different nationalities.

The process of integration is usually spread over several years. A company taken over keeps a degree of independence for some time, and is later fully integrated into the group structure, as old product names disappear, factories close down, and managers are more and more often appointed by head office.

There will often be rivalries: one factory will think that its products are better than another's; the managing director of the firm taken over might resent becoming merely manager of a subsidiary; 'outsiders' from head office will have a hard time being accepted; and there could be a problem with languages in the event of an international amalgamation.

Outline of roles

A: President: irritated by uncooperative stance of British; determined to integrate group.

B: Marketing Manager, head office: gets little cooperation from British; suspects they want to keep his/her visits to a minimum; thinks the British should make more effort to learn French.

C: Managing Director, British subsidiary: resents head office interference; wants to preserve family atmosphere in Sheffield factory; doesn't want to learn French.

D: Director of Human Relations, head office: thinks language barrier is a problem; wants to concentrate on good industrial relations.

E: Marketing Manager, Sheffield: thinks it's a mistake to market Sheffield products alongside inferior products from Belgium and France; admits communications with Thiers are poor.

F: Industrial Manager: has difficulty getting any figures from Sheffield, and persuading British to change their working practices and improve productivity.

G: Production Manager, Sheffield plant: thinks French should clean up their own factory and improve industrial relations in Thiers before criticizing British plant.

H: Plant Manager, Bruges plant: delighted to belong to a European group and cannot understand why the British do not feel the same way.

Possible outcome

There are no clear-cut answers, as this is a complicated issue of opposing positions. It is unlikely that the British will suddenly accept they are wrong to be uncooperative, that they should improve their French, or that their products are not really better than the other factories. It is equally unlikely that the French parent company will not continue to try to fully integrate the British into their group, even to the extent of putting their own managers in to get the cooperation they want. Perhaps the best that can be achieved is some kind of compromise; what that is will depend on how well individuals argue their cases.

If all the roles are used, the most serious argument might well be about marketing strategy. The French would seem to have a point when they say the best thing is to take advantage of the European dimension of the group and market all the group products in the different countries. And yet the British might well be right that their up-market products should not be associated with cheaper products from France and Belgium.

Vocabulary

autonomy: independence

to break into (a market): to get a share of, to start selling goods in

to contract out: to pay an outside firm to provide goods or services

cutlery: knives, forks and spoons for eating with

daft: silly, stupid

integration: bringing together, harmonizing, joining, uniting

interference: intrusion, intervention

language barrier: inability to communicate because you don't speak the same language

to lay off: to stop employing your workers, usually because of lack of work

to prowl: to move around looking for something to catch

running: management

set-up: situation

silverware: articles made of silver

stainless steel: steel which doesn't rust

stance: attitude

subsidiary: a company owned and controlled by another company

to take over: to buy, to take control of, a company

up-market: at the top end of the market, the best quality

working practices: the way work is organized, that goods are made

workforce: all the employees

New products

Introduction

1. 'Companies bring out new products because there is a market for them.' Do you agree? Can you think of other reasons why new products are put on the market? Make a list of reasons with your partner.

2. Which department in a company usually takes the initiative in bringing out new products: R and D, marketing, or the financial department?

3. What aspects have to be considered when bringing out a new product? With a partner, rank the following in order of importance (1 = the most important):

☐ Technology
(Have you developed a reliable, innovative, quality product?)

☐ Production
(Do you have enough production facilities, space, qualified workers and machinery?)

☐ Competition
(Are you the first on the market with this product? How soon will competitors bring out a similar product? How strong is the competition?)

☐ Finance
(What investment is needed? Will the company increase profits with the new product?)

☐ Marketing
(Are you breaking into new markets? How will you advertise?)

☐ Outlets and Distribution
(Can you use existing retailers or do you need to find new ones? Can you get the product to them easily?)

Now compare your list with the rest of the group.

Photocopiable

Business Roles
New products

© Cambridge
University Press
1997

New products

Situation

You work for the Nigerian Battery Company (NBC), which has two factories in Lagos. Your company is the largest lead-acid battery manufacturer in West Africa: you have about a quarter of the 'renewal market' (when car owners change their battery), and nearly a third of the 'original equipment market' (supplying car manufacturers with batteries for new cars). Currently you supply batteries to Peugeot in Nigeria, Nissan in the Ivory Coast, Toyota in Ghana, and Volkswagen in Cameroon.

Like every company, you want to increase your turnover. However, from a sales point of view your problem is that you can't very easily increase sales in either of your markets with your current products: car manufacturers don't want to be over-dependent on any one supplier, and on the renewal market competition is very fierce.

You are all agreed that the only way forward for NBC is to produce new products, possibly for new and different markets; however, you do not agree at all on *which* products to bring out.

You must decide:

- which sorts of new products should you produce and sell, to break into new markets and to increase the turnover and profits of NBC?

Business Roles
New products

© Cambridge
University Press
1997

Nigerian Battery Company:
product diversification flow chart

It is difficult for NBC to increase sales of car batteries. To expand and increase profits, we have decided to bring out a new product.
The options are:

We could choose lead-acid batteries similar to the car batteries we already make:
either

or

We can opt for batteries for small electric vehicles (cars, vans, etc.): these could be made from either

Stand-by batteries for tele-communications, computers and alarm systems

or

Motive power batteries for forklift trucks or luggage trucks at airports

Lead-acid, which is at least four times cheaper than nickel-cadmium

or

Nickel cadmium, which is lighter, more compact and more durable than lead-acid

Business Roles
New products

© Cambridge
University Press
1997

Role: **The Chief executive**

a

Chairing the meeting: You chair the meeting, make sure everyone speaks, and try to come to a collective agreement, failing which you yourself will have to decide. Organize the meeting in the following way:

1. Get each participant to give his or her opinion.

2. Make a list on the board of the different proposals.

3. Debate each proposal before coming to a decision.

Your own point of view: You are worried about moving into new areas, and would really like to continue only lead-acid battery production; however, you are ready to listen to your colleagues' arguments and consider them all.

Role: **The Director of Research**

b

You are against marketing new lead-acid products, and are in favour of nickel cadmium batteries.

You keep in close touch with car manufacturers, and you know that the future lies in electric vehicles. You are in the advanced stages of developing a nickel cadmium battery which has the advantages of light weight and long life. You have piloted one version on a small electric car in cooperation with

Volkswagen, and the results are very promising.

By contrast you think lead-acid batteries are too heavy, too bulky, need recharging too frequently, and have too short a lifespan, especially in the tropics.

Role: **The Director of Development**

You have been working, together with Peugeot in Nigeria, on a solar-powered electric car. You are confident that within two years you will be able to market your new design lead-acid battery for this vehicle. The main problem you needed to solve was the weight of the batteries in an otherwise extremely lightweight vehicle. You have new plates for inside the battery which

are made with a new light lead alloy and which are twice as thin as the plates you use at present. Your new battery is very promising, and you are convinced that it could be used in any type of car, not just electric cars. It is 25% lighter than existing batteries but would only cost about 10% more to manufacture.

Role: **The Marketing Manager**

C You feel this decision is really for you to make, as you know the market better than anyone else present.

You think the company should continue to produce only lead-acid batteries, as it has no knowledge of other types of battery. You agree that the car battery market cannot easily be developed, but there are infinite possibilities in the realm of motive power batteries and stand-by batteries. Enormous investment is going into telecommunications and computers in several West and Central African countries, and all the stand-by batteries for these uses are imported from Europe or Japan. There is equally a good market for motive power batteries for such things as forklift trucks and airport baggage trucks. Again, all these products are at present imported.

All your know-how is in the lead-acid business, and you could actually use exactly the same raw materials, production methods and production facilities for manufacturing your new products as you use at present for car batteries.

Role: **The Production Manager**

 You agree that your new products should be in the lead-acid field, but think you should be very careful, for two reasons:

- the market for stand-by batteries is big and growing, but it is dominated by Japanese and other Far Eastern manufacturers, and it would be difficult for you to compete with them

- your production facilities could not easily be adapted to making other sorts of batteries. Both your factories in Lagos work three shifts, seven days a week: when and how could you halt production of car batteries to make other sorts?

However, although it would mean investing in new plant, you think there is a good market in Africa for lead-acid batteries for pumps and industrial vehicles, and why not eventually for solar-powered electric cars?

Role: **The Financial Controller**

f

You are worried about the cost of the proposals. You want to be sure that bringing out new products will really increase profits. Can your colleagues really guarantee that their different suggestions will not lead to over-spending on research, new machinery, or trying to break into new markets? You are particularly concerned about the financial burden of building a new factory, so the only solution which will get your support is one which will not involve this kind of investment, but which would ensure that you can use existing production facilities as much as possible.

Role : **The Personnel Manager**

This whole idea of bringing out new products is a difficult problem for you. Both your factories in Lagos work three shifts a day, seven days a week, so you are sure that bringing out new products would mean building a new factory. It is not easy for you to keep skilled or semi-skilled operators for the existing factories, and things could only be worse if you had another factory. As for managerial staff, you have a problem getting them to join your company: not enough local people are sufficiently qualified, and some foreigners are reluctant to come to Nigeria because of the climate and living conditions.

Role: **The Original Equipment Sales Manager**

You are regularly in contact with all the car manufacturers that you supply with batteries for new cars. You are following closely developments both at Peugeot and at Volkswagen.

You think that the lightweight lead-acid battery is a better option for your company, because it would involve few changes to the production process. However, Peugeot are certain to want you to sell the battery only to them, at least initially.

The nickel cadmium battery is terribly expensive both to develop and produce, but would have the advantage of being much lighter than the lead-acid battery, and once Volkswagen had brought out their new car, you'd be able to sell it to all vehicle manufacturers.

New products

In brief

The Nigerian Battery Company, based in Lagos, produces lead-acid batteries for the car market. It needs to bring out new products and to break into new markets: the most obvious choice is lead-acid batteries for other uses, but some participants have other and more radical ideas.

Structure and procedure of the simulation

Introduction (optional) – 10-15 minutes

Preparation – 20-30 minutes

Simulation – 45-75 minutes

Follow-up (optional) – 15-20 minutes

Introduction

The statement in question 1 is the 'obvious' reason for bringing out new products; the aim here is to find the less obvious reasons. Ask learners to think about it with their partner and to make a short list of reasons. (See 'Business background' for suggested answers.)

In question 2, the motivators who push for new products to be brought out will vary from company to company and market to market. Experience shows it is often the marketing people; however, as this simulation shows, other people from other departments will always be involved too.

For question 3, ask learners to work with their partner again and decide which are the key points to consider when a company is bringing out a new product; they should rank them in order of importance. When they have completed their ranking, ask the pairs to compare their ranking with other pairs in the group.

The ranking here is designed to encourage discussion, at the same time as giving ideas to the learners about the problems involved in bringing out new products. They may well find it difficult to agree amongst themselves; in fact, the different aspects of the question are inseparable, and all influence the decision and ability to bring out new products. For example, if a company has an innovation to market but no money to finance it, the project will collapse.

Preparation

See the section 'General notes for teachers', p 2, for details on preparing learners for the simulation.

Simulation

See the section 'General notes for teachers', p 2, for details on managing the simulation.

Follow-up

See the section 'General notes for teachers', p 2, for details on feedback techniques and evaluation.

Summary of story

A Nigerian manufacturer of lead-acid batteries for cars wants to bring out new products. There are different possibilities: lead-acid batteries for uses other than cars (telecommunications, computers, forklift trucks, luggage handling vehicles, solar pumps); a new lightweight lead-acid battery for electric cars; or nickel cadmium batteries for electric vehicles. It is not a simple choice, and is complicated by the question of whether it is necessary or desirable to build a new factory for the new products.

Business background

Companies regularly launch new products. In many cases, it is because their competitors do so, and they need to keep up and avoid losing market share (e.g. products such as perfumes, yoghurts, washing powders, even cars). Sometimes they have a new type of product to market, maybe a technical innovation. And often it is simply to diversify, to avoid being over-dependent on one product or one type of product. In addition, manufacturers they supply their products to, such as car makers, will usually try to avoid being over-dependent on any supplier: this is why the Nigerian Battery Company cannot easily increase its already good market share of supplies to car manufacturers. The factor of over-dependence is the main reason for launching a new product in this simulation, though technical innovation might also play a role.

Outline of roles

A: Chief Executive: would prefer to keep to lead-acid batteries.

B: Director of Research: in favour of nickel cadmium batteries for electric vehicles.

C: Marketing Manager: wants to stay with lead-acid batteries, and get into stand-by and motive power markets.

D: Production Manager: would prefer lead-acid batteries. Thinks firm will need new factory, but could get new markets for pumps, industrial vehicles and solar-powered electric cars.

E: Director of Development: has designed lightweight lead-acid battery for solar-powered electric car.

F: Financial Controller: against costly solutions; wants to keep to lead-acid products and so use existing production facilities.

G: Personnel Manager: knows firm will need new factory, and thinks it'll be hard to find operators and managers.

H: Original Equipment Sales Manager: sees advantages in developing either nickel cadmium battery or lightweight lead-acid battery.

Possible outcome

The case for developing nickel cadmium batteries might be a good one, but the Director of Research is unlikely to have support for this when so many favour developing lead-acid batteries. If he or she is very good, they might be able to persuade the others, but it's improbable.

The lightweight lead-acid battery might be chosen, again depending on how convincing its supporter, the Director of Development, is. The answer to the question of what products to develop does not just depend on the technical aspects, but also on how good a market electric vehicles might become in the future as opposed to how good the market is for stand-by or motive power batteries.

In conclusion, the possible outcome is very open, and you are unlikely to have two groups coming to the same conclusions.

Vocabulary

bulky: big (implies too big)

development: work to improve existing products and materials

forklift truck: a small vehicle which lifts and transports goods around factories and warehouses

know-how: knowledge and expertise

lifespan: how long something lasts

to move into new fields: to try something new

to pilot: to test or experiment

raw materials: the basic materials from which products are made

research: work to make new products and materials

semi-skilled: having some ability to do a job, but less than a skilled worker

(day, evening, night) shift: a specific period of work time during the day or night when some workers work

skilled operator: a worker who has a particular skill

solar-powered: powered by the sun

supplier: person or firm who provides goods to a factory, warehouse or shop

turnover: total business done by a company in a given period

Flexible working time

Introduction

1. What are your working hours? (If you are not working now, what were your working hours in your last job?)

2. Do/Did they suit you? Why (not)?

3. Have you ever heard of 'flexitime', a system of flexible working hours? Can you explain how the system works (perhaps in your own company)?

4. If you do have flexitime in your company, do you think it is a good system? Is there anything about it you would like to change?

5. If you don't have flexitime in your company, or you're not working at the moment, what sort of flexitime system would you propose as the ideal system?

Business Roles
Flexible working time

© Cambridge University Press 1997

Flexible working time

Situation

You work for the Fabryka Samochodow Polskich, a car manufacturer which has its head office and main factory in Poznan, Poland. This company was recently taken over by a major Italian car builder, and you are now making one of their models for European markets.

Since the takeover, a problem of communication has arisen between the parent company's offices in Turin, Italy, and your offices in Poznan. This is because you do not have exactly the same working hours. In your offices in Poland, your current working hours are:

7.30 a.m. – work starts

9.30 a.m. – 20-minute tea break

12 noon to 12.30 p.m. – lunch break

2.30 p.m. – 20-minute tea break

4 p.m. – work finishes

You work a five-day week, so total working time per week amounts to 36 hours and 40 minutes. Many employees, particularly working parents, find these times convenient, as it avoids leaving children alone at home after school for too long: in Poland, some younger children go to school only in the morning, and others only in the afternoon, and many older children finish their school day as early as 2 or 3 p.m.

Today you are meeting to discuss this communication problem. The introduction of a system of flexible working time is being proposed as a solution. As the parent company thinks you do not work long enough hours in Poland, they also wish to incorporate an increase in total working time into the new arrangements. (These problems do not concern the factory, which has a completely different work system.)

You must decide:

• whether the introduction of flexible working time will solve the communication problems

• if it could, exactly what system should be used

• if it is acceptable to increase the total number of hours worked

---

Business Roles
Flexible working time

© Cambridge University Press 1997

Role: **The Managing Director**

a

Chairing the meeting: You chair the meeting. You ensure that everyone participates, and that decisions are reached today. Organize the meeting in the following way:

1. First, discuss exactly what the communication problems with Turin are.

2. Could the introduction of a flexible system solve them? Ask each participant to make specific proposals for a time schedule for this new system, and write them on the board.

3. Then discuss the positive and negative points of each proposal, again noting the main arguments on the board.

Your point of view: You are an Italian, and only recently took over management of the Polish subsidiary. You are very surprised by work practices in the head office in Poznan, and are determined to change them.

The main thing you want to change is the total number of hours worked. This is eight hours a day at the moment, and includes tea breaks. You feel that either the breaks should be abolished or forty minutes should be added to the working day, so that the staff actually *work* eight hours.

Because of the communication problems with the Turin office, you think that a system of flexible working time is essential. You don't really mind what time schedule is adopted, and are quite ready to listen to your colleagues' arguments and be flexible.

Role: **The Trade Union Representative**

c

Your aim is to ensure that the interests of the workers are really taken into account. You know that they will be very unhappy about the introduction of any new scheme if the real aim is simply to increase the number of hours worked, without any increase in pay. They will be especially unhappy if they lose their tea breaks, which are important to them.

You feel that it is vital that if a new system is brought in, it will still be possible for people to leave work early if they want. It must be remembered that many children finish school at 2 or 3 p.m., and parents need to get home to look after them.

Role: **The Personnel Manager**

You strongly support a flexible working time arrangement. This is what you would suggest:

work starts – between 7.30 a.m. and 9 a.m.

tea break – free tea between 10 a.m. and 11 a.m., work continues without break

lunch break – minimum of 45 minutes, taken between 11.45 a.m. and 1.15 p.m.

tea break – free tea between 3 p.m. and 4 p.m., work continues without break

work ends – between 4 p.m. and 6 p.m.

standard number of hours to be worked per week – 37.5

one day off per month for 7.5 hours overtime worked in previous month

The advantages of this system would be:

- employees wouldn't have to work more hours, despite losing their tea breaks

- they could if they so wished continue to work about the same times as at present; they could also arrive much later in the morning, take a longer lunch break, and leave later in the evening

- the day off every month would be very motivating

Business Roles
Flexible working time

© Cambridge University Press 1997

Role: **The Personal Assistant (PA) to the Managing Director**

You are in charge of all the secretarial staff in head office, and want their needs and desires to be taken into account.

You are ready to consider change, as a flexible system might help parents to be at home more often to look after their children when they are not at school, or to be more available for taking their children to school or collecting them from school. The new system will therefore need to be very flexible if it is to be an improvement for employees: for example, some employees might wish to be free as early as 2 or 3 p.m.

some days. Point out to the meeting that at present, if an employee arrives late because the train was late or a child is ill, they do not have to make up the lost time. A flexible time system would force people to work the full week in all circumstances.

Try to convince your colleagues that flexible working time will only be welcomed by the staff if it can be seen to make life easier for them. It must not be an excuse for working harder or longer.

Business Roles
Flexible working time

© Cambridge University Press 1997

Role: **The Marketing Manager**

You support a change to flexitime. You have one of the most important jobs in the company, and always work late. Unfortunately, with present working times, all your assistants and secretaries disappear at four o'clock sharp. You would be delighted if some of them were able to choose to arrive later in the morning, or take a longer lunch hour, and then be around to help at five or six in the evening.

Having such a short lunch break doesn't suit you either. You often have to take customers out to lunch, and don't get back until two-thirty or three o'clock – so why not let your employees take a long break as well?

Business Roles
Flexible working time

© Cambridge University Press 1997

Role: **The Communications Manager**

Your wish is naturally to improve internal communications with the factories and the Italians, and external communications with suppliers, distributors and customers.

The factories work three shifts, and only the morning shift has easy contact with head office. There's not much you can do to help communications with the night shift, but if some head office workers worked later in the afternoon and evening it would help communications with the evening shift.

You find it is hard to get in touch with your Italian counterparts at lunchtime, and you know they are often irritated by the absence of head office staff in Poznan after 4 p.m.

In fact, your rather rigid working times cause communication problems with practically all your international contacts. It is only convenient within Poland, where everyone tends to work to similar schedules and similar constraints.

Business Roles
Flexible working time

© Cambridge University Press 1997

Flexible working time

In brief

A Polish car company has recently been taken over by a major Italian car manufacturer. Communications between the Polish head office in Poznan and the parent company in Turin are being disrupted by the Poles' incompatible working hours: an early start, an early finish, a very short lunch break, and long tea breaks. Today's meeting is to discuss the possible introduction of a system of flexible working time for the staff at head office to overcome this problem.

Structure and procedure of the simulation

Introduction (optional) – 15-20 minutes

Preparation – 10-20 minutes

Simulation – 30-40 minutes

Follow-up (optional) – 15-20 minutes

Introduction

These questions are designed to encourage group discussion on the topic of flexitime. Ask any managers in the group (who probably don't work fixed hours) to talk about their staff's hours. Pre-work learners might like to talk about placements or holiday jobs, but in the absence of any work experience, concentrate on questions 3 and 5.

See 'Business background' for information about flexitime.

Preparation

See the section 'General notes for teachers', p 2, for details on preparing learners for the simulation.

Note: Ensure that the role of union representative is given to a student capable of sustaining their argument, as they are the only person with serious doubts about flexitime. The Managing Director is Italian and all the other participants Polish, which is why the discussion is in English.

Simulation

See the section 'General notes for teachers', p 2, for details on managing the simulation.

Follow-up

See the section 'General notes for teachers', p 2, for details on feedback techniques and evaluation.

Summary of story

Today's meeting is to discuss the introduction of flexible working time and a possible increase in the hours worked in the head office of a Polish car manufacturer, recently taken over by an Italian car maker based in Turin.

Because of their current working hours – early start, short lunch break and early finish – and the Italian practice of long lunches, communications with Italy are difficult: at lunchtime the Poles cannot get hold of their Italian counterparts in Turin, and late afternoon it's the same problem the other way round.

In addition, the Polish staff take two twenty-minute tea breaks morning and afternoon, meaning they actually work only seven hours and twenty minutes a day instead of the full eight hours – something the new Italian managing director does not approve of and wants to abolish.

Some staff are worried about having to work more hours, and will only favour a change to flexitime if it makes it easier for them to look after their children after school.

Business background

Flexible working time, or 'flexitime', is common in many countries now. There are different systems, but they are usually based on a common principle of a compulsory working period, sometimes called 'coretime', and a more flexible working period running from the earliest normal starting time for work to the latest normal finishing time, called ' bandtime'. Flexitime is the period of bandtime outside of coretime. So for example, a company may have a bandtime of 8 a.m. to 7 p.m. and a coretime of 9.30-11a.m. and 2-4p.m.; this means that a worker can start work any time from 8-9.30a.m., take a lunch break for a period between 11a.m. and 2p.m., and leave any time after 4p.m. and before 7p.m. Hours worked are recorded daily, and the worker is still required to work a set number of hours in a week or month: the flexibility is that they can, to some extent, choose when those working hours are.

Where systems differ is in the 'perks' connected to the system, in particular concerning the amount of time you can take off once you have worked over your set number of hours. This varies from a rather mean nothing at all, obliging you to do exactly the number of hours laid down per month or per week, with flexibility only in how many you do each day, to a very generous day off a week, meaning you can work a four-day week if you so choose. This is rare, but one to two days off a month is quite common.

How flexitime works can depend a lot on local factors, for example, whether people usually take a long lunch break or not. It is said that in Europe the further south you go, the longer the lunch break is!

Outline of roles

A: Managing Director: is Italian, and worried about communication problems with Italian head office; thinks flexitime is essential, and wants to get rid of tea breaks.

B: Personnel Manager: has a flexitime system all worked out, with arguments in favour.

C: Union Representative: concerned that scheme is a way to increase the number of hours worked by employees, and about the potential loss of tea breaks.

D: PA to Managing Director: wants to defend interests of secretarial staff; would like staff to be able to arrive later or leave earlier if necessary; sees possible drawbacks in flexitime.

E: Marketing Manager: wants new system enabling employees to be in the office after 4 p.m.; also wants longer lunch break.

F: Communications Manager: thinks longer lunch break and later working hours would help international communications.

Possible outcome

The conflict will be between those who want to increase the number of hours worked and have more flexible working times so that staff are more available for communications with Turin, particularly after 4 p.m., and those who want to resist the increase, and will only favour flexitime if it enables parents to be more available to look after their children after school. You can expect some form of flexitime to be adopted as there is not a lot of opposition to it, but this might only be if it is possible, for those who want to, to leave work even earlier than at present.

Vocabulary

(tea, lunch) break: a period of time when you stop work for a rest and a drink or food

counterpart: someone who does a similar job to yours, in another place

a day off: a free day from work

flexible working time, flexitime: a system allowing employees some flexibility in their working hours

overtime: time worked in addition to your usual working hours

parent company: a company which owns and controls a subsidiary company by holding more than half its shares

(day, evening, night) shift: a specific period of work time during the day or night when some workers work

to take over: to buy, to take control of, a company

Business Roles
**Flexible working
time**

The head office

Introduction

Your firm is considering whether or not to find a new location for its head office and, if so, where it should be. Members of the board of management have different opinions on the subject. Read their opinions and, with a partner, number them in order of importance (1 = most important):

☐ 'We need new offices to make it more pleasant for staff to work there.'

☐ 'We should move to an area where office rents are cheaper.'

☐ 'It would be a good idea to build the head office next to one of our factories.'

☐ 'I really don't want to move away from here. I've just had a new house built.'

☐ 'We ought to move closer to residential areas, to shorten employees' travel time to work.'

☐ 'Communications are all-important: we must find somewhere near a motorway, an airport and a railway station.'

☐ 'Where the head office is determines the quality of the image the public have of the company. We need to move somewhere nice, even if it's expensive.'

☐ 'We should move to a place with more sunshine.'

☐ 'We must be in a big city centre, close to our competitors, customers, banks and suppliers.'

☐ 'We must move to a small provincial town, where life is more relaxed and we can work efficiently.'

Now compare your list with the rest of the class and explain your choices.

Business Roles
The head office

© Cambridge
University Press
1997

The head office

Situation

You work for PBC, the Plastic Bottle Company. After some difficult years at the beginning of the nineties, the firm is now profitable again. The company has five factories in England and Wales, two in continental Europe and a workforce of nearly 3,000. It is the European market leader, but there are 15 other major competitors in Europe. It is unknown to the general public, but has large contracts with all the main makers of mineral water, non-alcoholic drinks, and household products.

The company is divided into two divisions:

The Household Products Division – this makes bottles for products like washing-up liquid and bleach, at factories in Swansea in Wales, Manchester and Birmingham in England, and Aalkmaar in Holland.

The Drinks Division – this produces bottles for non-alcoholic drinks and mineral water, at factories in Swindon and Maidstone in England and Odense in Denmark.

Your head office is located in New Cross, in the inner suburbs of London. The building is rather dull and dirty – in fact it is an old factory, which ceased production about fifteen years ago.

When a new managing director took over two years ago, the first promise they made was that a new head office would be found within a year. Since then, nothing much has been done about the problem. Today, a meeting of managers has been called to discuss the problem.

You must decide:

• if you need a new head office

• if you do, whether it would be better to:
– build a new office on the present site
– find new offices somewhere else
– have new offices specially built somewhere else

Business Roles
The head office

© Cambridge
University Press
1997

Possible locations for PBC's head office

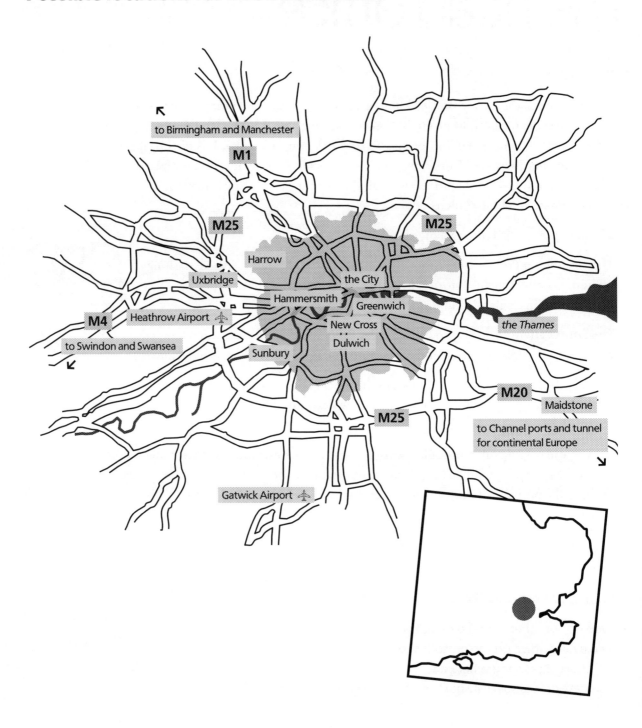

Business Roles
The head office

© Cambridge
University Press
1997

Role: **The Managing Director**

Chairing the meeting: Make sure that everyone joins in and gives their opinion. Organize the meeting in the following way:

1. Debate the question of whether you really need a new head office first.

2. Then discuss possible locations.

3. If you decide to move, list up on the board the different locations suggested with the pros and cons of each.

Your own point of view: You promised to find new offices within a year of taking up your job. You wanted to build new offices on the present site, as the company owns the land, and you think New Cross is a convenient place to work, near the City, near the motorway to Maidstone, Dover and the continent, and near your home in Greenwich.

Unfortunately, planning permission was refused by the local council, and since then you have been too busy trying to reduce costs in the factories, increase productivity, and take over competitors; you have taken over firms in Holland and Denmark in the last year, and are interested in a firm in Spain.

You really want a solution which will not be costly for the firm, and which will enable you personally to continue working in the area and not have to move from your lovely house in Greenwich.

Role: **The Communications Manager**

You have recently joined the company, and feel that it is imperative for the corporate image of the firm that you move to new and modern offices as soon as possible. You are fed up with working in a dark little office on the third floor, with your secretary on the second floor.

You live in Harrow, on the other side of London from the offices in New Cross. Although it's possible for you to get to work by tube, it takes a very long time. You don't really mind where the new head office is, so long as there is one, and soon. But you think it would be best for the image of the company if you went to somewhere like Uxbridge, which is a modern town, with offices readily available, near Heathrow airport and several motorways, including the M4 to South Wales, and, of course, near your home.

Role: **The Marketing Manager, Household Products Division**

c You feel a very strong need for a new head office. You are ashamed of your drab office, and try to avoid inviting work associates to headquarters because of this. What's more, someone from the advertising agency you use was recently mugged coming out of New Cross Station, and you would really like to find offices in a decent area.

You think the company should look for offices in somewhere like Hammersmith. Then you would be close to the centre of London, near Heathrow Airport, and near the motorway to the west of England and to Wales, where you have a household products factory. You admit that this would be costly, but feel it should be looked on as an investment in marketing and public relations terms.

Business Roles
The head office

© Cambridge
University Press
1997

Role: **The Marketing Manager, Drinks Division**

d You are the marketing manager of the Drinks Division. You think the old and dirty offices in New Cross should be replaced by new purpose-built headquarters on the present site. As a marketing person, you are ashamed of the state of your workplace, and are convinced you have lost business through having to welcome visitors there. Just last year, you lost an important contract with Pepsi-Cola when their representative had a stomach upset after eating in your canteen.

There is a lot of rivalry between the two divisions in your company. You know this is childish, but are still fed up with the Household Division causing problems. The reason planning permission was refused last time for your new offices was that the council wanted to build a new road through the site, and was only willing to give planning permission for two separate office blocks, one on each side of the road. You think this is a great idea, as you could have offices which were completely separate from the Household Division's.

Business Roles
The head office

© Cambridge
University Press
1997

Role: **The Production Manager, Drinks Division**

You are in charge of production in the factories in Swindon, Maidstone and Denmark. You really can't see the need for a new head office. You were hoping that a new factory would be built in Maidstone, and think that if the company has money to spend, it should be spent on that, or on taking over the Spanish firm you know the managing director is interested in.

You travel a lot, but find New Cross really quite convenient for getting to Maidstone, or to Gatwick Airport to fly to Denmark. You have just bought a new house in Dulwich, and wouldn't like to have to move now.

Role: **The Production Manager, Household Products Division**

You are in charge of production in the three household products factories in Swansea, Manchester and Birmingham. You are trying to integrate the Dutch factory into your division, and so make frequent visits to Holland, but it is still not really clear whether you or the managing director of the Dutch subsidiary are in charge.

You have worked for PBC for 25 years, and can't understand why anyone should want to move head office. You have plenty of room for expansion, as the old production area is lying empty. You agree that the offices are rather drab, but think a good coat of paint would do the job, and would be much cheaper than moving. You feel company money should be invested in improving factory productivity, and wonder what has happened to the idea of building the new factory in Maidstone, which was discussed last year but then dropped when the Dutch company was taken over.

Role: **The Director of Human Relations**

g

You think that the company should have a new head office as soon as possible. You try to motivate your employees as much as you can, but you find it very difficult, as you work in such old, dark and dismal offices.

In your opinion, the company should move away from New Cross, as it's a poor and run-down area, and it's difficult for you to find employees with the right qualifications living near head office. What's more, it's difficult to get well-qualified staff to come to New Cross, as they tend to live in the western suburbs of London, and don't like travelling such a long time each day.

You have recently been told about some very nice offices available in Sunbury, and think that would be the ideal location for a new head office. To add to that, your husband/wife was brought up in Sunbury, and is keen to move back.

Role: **The Financial Manager**

h

You have rather mixed feelings about the idea of a move. You have been with the company for thirty years and like working in New Cross. On the other hand you know that employees generally like neither the present offices nor New Cross, and that eventually you will have to move. If a move has to be made, you favour building a new factory in Maidstone, which could be the new head office as well.

The best solution for you would be to stay in New Cross until you retire in two years' time. So you argue that no decision should be taken for the time being, on the grounds that it would be better to concentrate on integrating the new factories in Holland and Denmark, and that any money the company has available at the moment should be spent on the takeover of the Spanish firm.

Role: **The Head of Research and Development**

i

You do your R and D in New Cross. The buildings are really quite suitable for that, as they used to be a factory. You have to admit, however, that people don't like coming to work in this area, and you have difficulty attracting suitably qualified staff.

The best solution for you would be purpose-built premises, and you think these could be integrated into the new factory in Maidstone which was being planned a couple of years ago. You don't particularly want to go to Maidstone, though, and think it might be easier to find the right staff in west London.

The head office

In brief

The Plastic Bottle Company, which manufactures bottles for products like non-alcoholic drinks and washing-up liquid, is thinking of moving to a new head office. The present offices are in an old factory, which is a rather dull, dirty building in the inner suburbs of London. Today's meeting is to decide if new offices are needed, and, if so, where they should be located.

Structure and procedure of the simulation

Introduction *(optional)* – 15-20 minutes

Preparation – 15-20 minutes

Simulation 30-60 minutes

Follow-up *(optional)* – 15-20 minutes

Introduction

This task is designed as an introduction to the subject of relocation, and is particularly suited to those learners who may have no idea of what the choice of a new head office involves.

The first part of the task can be done in twos or threes; the learners can help each other to understand the exact meanings of the opinions, and then discuss together in what order of importance they will classify the different propositions. They will probably agree that a reason like 'moving to a place with more sunshine' is at the bottom of the list, whereas being 'near a motorway, an airport and a railway station' will be near the top.

After that work as a class, compare lists, and get learners to explain why they attach importance to a given opinion. Keep discussion short, remembering that the main discussion will be during the simulation itself.

Preparation

See the section 'General notes for teachers', p 2, for details on preparing learners for the simulation.

The map should also be copied and given out to the learners. It shows the current location of the PBC head office, and the locations under consideration for the new head office.

Simulation

See the section 'General notes for teachers', p 2, for details on managing the simulation.

Follow-up

See the section 'General notes for teachers', p 2, for details on feedback techniques and evaluation.

Summary of story

The Plastic Bottle Company has to decide if it needs to find a new head office. The present office is an old and dirty disused factory situated in New Cross, an inner suburb of London, England. Today's discussion will be firstly about the need for a new head office, and then about a possible location if the decision is made to move.

If the decision is made to move away from New Cross, the candidates, if all roles are used, will be: Maidstone, which is a town to the south-east of London, Sunbury, a town to the south-west of London, Uxbridge, west of London and Hammersmith in west London.

Most participants want to move west of London, where the majority of employees live, and where communications might be better because of motorway links to the company's British factories, such as the M1 motorway to Birmingham. Being based in the west also means being near Heathrow Airport, one of London's main airports. But they are not in agreement as to which place!

To complicate matters, a few people don't see the need to move at all. They argue that New Cross is perfectly convenient for communications with the City of London, Gatwick (London's other main airport), and the company's other factories in Holland and Denmark.

Business background

This is a serious topic. The location of the head office might change the whole future of a company because of its effect on the image or the quality of the workforce. The Introduction will give you and your students precise ideas as to why companies might decide to change the location of their head office.

Many head offices are in their present location for no particular reason. It is not often that the decision is made to move. Some companies do move for reasons of image, convenience, quality, worker motivation or communications. Others might simply move somewhere where they own land to build on, where labour, taxes or rents are cheaper, or even to somewhere nearer the chief executive's home!

Outline of roles

A: Managing Director: quite satisfied with New Cross; wanted to build new offices there, but planning permission was refused.

B: Communications Manager: thinks it's imperative for image of company to find new offices; suggests Uxbridge, west of London.

C: Marketing Manager, Household Products Division: ashamed of present offices; proposes Hammersmith in west London as new location.

D: Marketing Manager, Drinks Division: wants new offices on present site in New Cross, with an office on each side of the road to keep the divisions apart.

E: Production Manager, Drinks Division: thinks New Cross is fine, and would rather money was spent on a new factory in Maidstone or on the Spanish takeover; in addition, has just bought a house in the area of present office and doesn't want to move.

F: Production Manager, Household Products Division: wants to keep present offices in New Cross which simply need a coat of paint; would rather money was spent on a new factory in Maidstone.

G: Director of Human Relations: wants to move and suggests Sunbury, south-west of London, where it should be possible to find suitable staff more easily.

H: Financial Manager: prefers staying in New Cross (at least until s/he retires in two years' time) and concentrating resources on subsidiary companies and on the Spanish takeover; if a move has to be made, favours a new factory and head office in Maidstone.

I: Head of R and D: has no very fixed ideas, but would possibly favour either building a new factory in Maidstone or relocating to west London.

Possible outcome

The participants will very probably choose to move to new offices in a new location. There is no clear favourite for this location, though the most likely choices are Hammersmith or Uxbridge, with Sunbury as an outsider. The idea of building a new factory in Maidstone and integrating a new head office into it is just a possibility.

Vocabulary

on the cards: probable, proposed, possible

dismal: miserable, depressing

to do the job: to achieve the result you want

drab: colourless, dull, shabby

dull: dismal, grey

fed up: annoyed by something you have experienced for too long

to have mixed feelings about something: to be unsure about something because you see both positive and negative aspects to it

motorway (BE): **freeway** (AmE)

to be mugged: to be attacked and robbed in the street

planning permission: official permission to build something new

purpose-built: specially built

run-down: in bad condition

to shelve: to delay something until a later time

stomach upset: illness of the stomach

tube: an underground train for suburban or city travel